Dash o Doric
ONE FOR THE ROAD

Dash o Doric

ONE FOR THE ROAD

Robbie Shepherd
and
Norman Harper

Birlinn

First published in Great Britain in 2004
by Birlinn Ltd
West Newington House
10 Newington Road
Edinburgh
EH9 1QS

www.birlinn.co.uk

ISBN 1 84158 324 3

British Library Cataloguing-in-Publication Data
A catalogue record for this book is available on request
from the British Library

Typeset by Palimpsest Book Production, Polmont, Stirlingshire
Printed and bound by Nørhaven Paperback A/S

To our wives, Esma and Alison, for their forbearance, but also to the many thousands of sons and daughters of the North-east who, like us, hold the culture, the area and the people dearest to their hearts

Contents

Foreword   viii

Babes and Sucklings   1
Sweet Bird of Doric Wit   11
Kissies and Bosies   20
The Shoppie   28
Doon on the Fairm   36
Characters   43
The Toon   53
The Papers   61
Aches and Pains   70
Law and Order   81
Please, Miss   88
Good for the Soul   99
Mony a Gweed Tune   107
Mixter Maxter   115
The Tales That Got Awa   122

Where Credit's Due   132

Foreword

IT HAS been nearly 10 years since *A Dash o Doric* appeared, and it has always surprised and delighted both of us when we have been approached, out and about, by readers who enjoyed the tales of North-east humour that appeared in it and in its sequel, *Anither Dash o Doric*. Sometimes, these readers have related amusing stories and experiences of their own. Funny though these have been, we have always resisted compiling a third volume, partly because we didn't want to overstay our welcome, but also because a book like this eats up a surprisingly large number of stories, and simply gathering them together and preparing them in sufficient numbers takes more time than you think.

However, the tales our readers shared were too good to waste, so both of us evolved a system of scribbling brief reminders of them in our respective wee notebooks. We both hoped to be able to produce another "Dash" book when the time was right and when we had accumulated enough material.

It has taken almost a decade, but here it is.

Production of *One For The Road* (or "Dash 3" as it became known in trade shorthand) has not been without its problems. For one thing, it is difficult enough to read our handwriting at the best of times, but when the notes of an especially good tale amount to just a couple of hieroglyphs from seven or eight years ago, the unravelling and the remembering tax the wee grey cells more than we're accustomed to nowadays.

We have managed to decipher many of these two-word scribbles and to recall the anecdotes to which they refer, but at least half a dozen funny stories have been lost because our hurried notes have defeated us despite our best efforts, so the mists of time have closed about them.

If anyone knows what tales were meant to accompany "Green Sweater", "Fired Plumber" and "Disguised Grandma", either of us would be pleased to hear from you. Who knows, they might appear in a fourth "Dash" a decade hence.

Finally, many people deserve our thanks. Our multitude of contributors we list at the back, but we would also to thank the team at Birlinn for their support, encouragement and patience, notably Neville Moir and Hugh Andrew, and also Graham Maclennan for his fine cover artwork and his cartoons, which you will find sprinkled throughout.

We had also better thank our wives, Esma and Alison, who were ultimately the judges of what should be included and what should not. We hope you think they made the right decisions and that, for a third time, you enjoy your book.

Norman Harper and Robbie Shepherd
Aberdeen, 2004

Babes and Sucklings

Even youngsters get in on the Doric-humour act, as this selection shows.

WHEN YVONNE CORMACK was a young working mum, she would often entrust her children to her retired father, who enjoyed looking after the two of them – Ian (7) and Pauline (5).

One evening, when Yvonne arrived home from work, she found her dad trying to teach Pauline how to tell the time. Pauline had been a quick study and was confident enough to try to test her grandfather to see if he knew as much as she now did.

Yvonne heard her ask: "And foo mony minutes in an oor, granda?"

"Sixty."

"And foo mony oors in a day?"

"Twinty-fower."

"And foo lang's a minute?"

"Weel, lass," Yvonne heard her dad say, "that depends fit side o the lavvie door ye're on."

TO ELGIN now, and the Duncan family. Ewen Duncan's seven-year-old, Carrie-Ann, astonished the family one Christmas when she asked, quite matter-of-factly: "Daddy, what's a prostitute?"

Ewen wrote: "We've always answered a straight question as honestly as we can, but this one flummoxed me. So I just said: 'That's someone who gets paid money to . . . be friendly.' She seemed perfectly happy with that and the rest of us sighed with relief.

"On the Saturday night after New Year, when my wife and I were going out for a works do, our usual babysitter came round. The first thing Carrie-Ann told her was: 'Daddy says you're a prostitute.'"

A KEEN Rangers fan got in touch to say that he and his wife had been discussing a piece of vandalism near their home in which an exceptionally rude four-letter word had been scrawled on a garage door.

Their five-year-old daughter had become interested in the conversation and inquired: "What was the bad word, mummy?"

"Don't you worry about that," Mummy said. "It's not a word we would use in this house."

The child thought for a moment. "Was it Poo?"

"No, it wasn't Poo. It just wasn't a very nice word. Don't you worry about it."

"Was it 'Bum'?"

"No, it wasn't 'Bum', either."

The child thought for a moment, then her face darkened.

"It wasn't 'Celtic', was it?"

SEVERAL YEARS ago, Alan Grant, of Kemnay, was driving towards Aberdeen with his son Ryan sitting in the back of the car, when they had to stop at a pedestrian crossing at Bucksburn.

The driver of the car behind hadn't noticed in time that Alan had stopped, and collided at about 15mph. "I checked Ryan was all right," Alan said, "then I got out to see the damage. It wasn't much apart from a cracked bumper and a smashed tail-light glass, but the other driver was decent enough to admit it was all her fault.

"Ryan was very quiet after we drove off, and I began to worry that maybe he had concussion, but he assured me he was feeling fine. After a good 10 minutes he asked what the lady and I had been talking about outside the car.

"I explained that we had been exchanging names to keep the insurance people happy. At that point, he became really upset, almost to the point of tears appearing, and said: 'So fit are ye caaed noo?'"

A CORRESPONDENT who signed herself only as "Betty" told us of her three-year-old daughter running screaming and crying downstairs.

The little girl's grandfather had been staying the night and she had just seen him shaving with his electric razor, which had thrown her into a tremendous panic.

"Fit's adee, quinie?" Betty asked.

Through sobs, the child replied: "Granda's ironin his face."

SOMETIMES, a child says exactly what you wish you could say yourself. At a Moray school's nativity play in 2002, while proud parents in the audience were brandishing camcorders and Instamatics, there was a silence, filled eventually by a four-year-old voice from the darkness saying clearly: "Mummy, this is just rubbish, isn't it?"

FARMER'S WIFE Jean Lorimer, from near Fraserburgh, said her seven-year-old had tugged at her apron one September morning and asked: "Mam, foo mony days tae Christmas?"

"I dinna ken," Jean said. "I suppose it must be aboot a hunner. Fit wye?"

"Well," said her daughter. "I wis jist winderin if it wis time for me tae start bein a good girl."

SPELLING IS a challenge for most youngsters, and it certainly was in a class being taught by Elizabeth McGregor, who now lives near Lossiemouth, but who recalled her time at a Deeside primary school, especially one afternoon when the class was stumped on spelling "dahlia".

"I always maintained it was best that the children used their own initiative to find out answers," Elizabeth wrote, "so when one wee boy asked how to spell dahlia, I said I wasn't sure. I wanted to see if he would go to the class dictionary himself and look it up."

The lad did exactly that, but then Elizabeth heard one of the other class nickums lean across to the dictionary lad as he studied and say: "Ye're wastin yer time. Spell it ony wye ye like. She disna ken hersel."

ONE EASTER in the 1970s, Marianne Taylor, of Broomhill Road, Aberdeen, was looking after her six-year-old grandson and discovered quickly that modern children needed constant activity. After all the outdoor activities had been exhausted, Marianne brought out a box of crayons and a pad of paper and set him to work at the kitchen table.

"It was blissfully quiet at last," she said, "so I peeped in on him and saw him working away furiously, tongue out at the corner of his mouth. I went in to congratulate him on being such a good little artist."

"Did you have crayons in the olden days?" he asked.

Marianne said she did, but that they weren't nearly as nifty as the ones he was using.

"No," he said, going back to his drawing. "Yours must have been black and white."

IT'S CHRISTMAS, and the spirit of the season has seized primary schools throughout the North-east. Lindy Cheyne recalled a nearby teacher asking her class to draw a Christmas card with a nativity scene. The teacher surveyed them all, but was puzzled by one young artist's rendition.

It certainly included the three wise men, the donkeys and the sheep, Joseph, Mary and a bright glow round the baby Jesus, but there was also a large brown blob in the background.

She asked the artist what this was supposed to represent and was told crisply: "That's the stable bear."

A NEW fire-and-brimstone minister had come to one of the wee kirks at St Combs in 1927. His services became notorious for the histrionics he displayed while he lectured his flock about their evil ways. He thumped the pulpit, stamped his feet, bawled, shouted, waved his hands and generally worked himself into a red-faced fury.

"Mam," one small boy was heard to whisper nervously in the middle of the congregation, "fit happens if he gets oot o his box?"

EILEEN LEIPER was a school nurse who did the rounds of wee country schools in mid-Aberdeenshire from the mid-1940s to the mid-1970s. Part of the examination of the children involved weighing them. At Fisherford, one six-year-old girl refused to step on the scales, much to the embarrassment of her rather ample mother.

"Come awa, quinie," the mother said. "It's jist scales. We've got scales at hame. Nithing tae be feart o. Ye've seen me usin oors. Jist you dee the same."

The little girl slowly left her mother's side, stepped on the scales then clapped her hands to her mouth, looked down and cried: "God Almichty!"

ALAN McALLISTER, from Ellon, had taken the family on holiday to Spain for a fortnight, but hadn't read the small print closely enough, and discovered on the first morning at the seaside that they were just a couple of hundred yards from a nudist beach.

"It wasn't so much the embarrassment," Ian said, "as the fact that my eight-year-old, Jordan, was just staring pop-eyed at three young blondes. My wife and I didn't know what to do or say."

"When the three lassies got up to leave, Jordan was studying them intensely and I thought: 'This is it; the father–son talk.'"

"Then he turned round and said: 'Dad?'"

"I said: 'Yes, Jordan?'"

"God Almighty"

"He said: 'Can I hae that can o Coke the ladies left?'"

KEITH COUPLE Kathleen and Eddie Robertson agreed to look after their eight-year-old grandson from Australia, Kyle, while Kyle's mum and dad went visiting relatives in other parts of the UK.

Kyle was a little upset at having left all his wee pals in Melbourne, so Kathleen and Eddie decided they would pull out all the stops and impress him with the best of northern Scotland.

They took him to Loch Ness and Applecross, nearly every castle in Aberdeenshire, the Cairngorms, fishing, harbours, dolphin-watching and everything else they could think of. By the end of the fortnight, the Robertsons were tired out.

When Kyle said he wanted to phone home and tell his best friend about his visit, Kathleen was secretly very proud. She dialled the number for him and left him in private, but just as she was closing the door and the call went through, she heard Kyle say: "Jamie? Guess what? My grandad can take out his teeth!"

HELEN MENNIE has a rich archive of tales from her days as a primary-school teacher. One of her favourites concerns wee Iain, aged eight, who came from a farm somewhere near King Edward. Helen noticed one day that he was not his usual self. When the other children went into the playground, Iain stayed behind at his desk, biting his lip.

Helen was cleaning the blackboard before she realised that he was still there.

"Not going outside to play, Iain?" she said.

"No."

"Is there something worrying you?"

"Aye."

"What would that be?"

"Ma faither. I gied him that bit o paper ye sent hame wi me last wikk."

"The results of your tests?"

"Aye."

"Was he not pleased?"

"I'm nae needin tae worry ye, Miss, bit he says if I dinna improve, somebody's gettin a skelpin."

ANOTHER OF Helen's tales concerns a note that one of her former colleagues received one morning. It was typed neatly and read: "Please excuse Ian from PE today and tomorrow. He hasn't been feeling very well lately and is under the doctor's car."

HELEN WAS concerned one year when it became apparent that, somehow, her Primary Four class had discovered the date of her birthday. It was clear something was up because of all the whispering and excitement just before playtime on the day in question. When the bell rang, four of them raced out and returned with an obviously home-made cake.

"I was genuinely touched that they should have gone to all that trouble," Helen wrote, "so naturally I thanked them and did all the usual bit about blowing out the candles and making a wish."

Helen was just at the point of cutting the cake

when one voice piped up at her side. "Miss, foo aul are ye onywye?"

"Oh," Helen said with a wee laugh, "I'm not far off 100."

The boy turned to his pal and said: "See? Telt ye."

YOUNG STEWART was a pupil at Cruden Bay Primary School and lost his gymshoes – a major trauma for a six-year-old. Despite the best efforts of his teacher, and with a great deal of angst on Stewart's part, the errant gimmies were nowhere to be found.

Ultimately facing a large pile of assorted footwear, teacher asked: "Stewart, what size were your gymshoes?"

Stewart looked at her, mystified, and replied: "The same size as ma feet."

YOUNG MUM Deirdre Black, of Banchory, was watching her six-year-old, Emily, drawing at the kitchen table, and was soon presented with a picture of an extremely large cat.

"That's an affa big cat, Emily," Deirdre said. "It's affa fat."

"It's nae fat, mam," Emily said. "It's gaun tae hae kittens. Look, I'll show ye." Emily began adding the kittens inside the cat's body.

Deirdre thought this would be an appropriate moment to prompt questions about nature's way. "And div ye ken foo the kittens got there?"

"Of course," Emily said. "I drew them."

Sweet Bird of Doric Wit

No teenage cynicism here. This chapter demonstrates that those awkward years still keep hold on the quirky sense of humour that the North-east bestows.

ONE TEACHER wrote to us reminiscing about her days in front of a classroom at Banff. In the days of school class photographs, not everyone was willing to have their picture taken, and it was the teacher's job to persuade shy pupils to do up their ties and sit down with their fellows and wring out a smile for the camera.

Sometimes, the persuasion demanded superhuman patience, and one stubborn 13-year-old simply refused to have anything to do with the picture.

"Just think how good it will be when you're a big boy and you have a photograph of yourself and everybody else in the class," the teacher said.

"You'll be able to show your own children and say: 'Look, there's Andrew; he's a doctor. Look, there's Eilidh; she's a dentist. Look, there's Ian; he's a farmer.'"

At which a voice piped up at her back: "Look, there's the teacher. She's deid."

WHEN COMPUTERS and the Internet were just becoming widespread in the mid-1990s, Ewen Paterson, of Bridge of Don, went home excitedly one day to explain that he had been pulling facts, figures and research from around the world, all from a desk at the local academy.

His grandfather, who happened to be visiting, was intrigued and sought more information.

Ewen explained that at the touch of a button he had contacted Mississippi, Denmark, Sydney and South Africa.

"Ach, that's nithing," said the old man. "Ilky nicht for years I put ma haun aneth the bed and got china."

TEENAGERS OFTEN treat their parents with barely concealed contempt, but Eunice Grant, now teaching in Elgin, adored her dad, George, throughout his life "because he was so funny".

George, a farmer, used to spin his children wildly implausible tales of how poor he and his parents were when he was growing up. These tales included being so poor that there was no money for sugar, so relatives would bring empty sugar bags to the house for him and his brothers to sniff; being so poor that they couldn't afford school books, so the children would be taken out for walks to read road signs; and being so poor that they couldn't afford shoes, so they had their feet painted black instead.

"My favourite, though," Eunice wrote, "was the time when he was supposedly left in the house on his own for a weekend as a young man."

George claimed he couldn't find anything to eat in the house, then, by pure chance, he happened to open a cupboard under the stairs at breakfast time and out tumbled a sumptuous spread of ham sandwiches, which he devoured eagerly.

A few hours later, when he was looking for a screwdriver, he opened a cupboard under the sink and there was a steaming hot flow of lentil soup which, again, he polished off quickly.

Finally, he was trying to mend a fuse and went to the fusebox above the front door. He opened it and out fell boxes of ice cream and tubs of jelly.

"Ye see," he told his wide-eyed daughters, "like I've aye telt ye, I nivver kent far ma next meal wis comin fae."

WHEN HE was a ganger for a sub-contractor at the Howard Doris yard at Kishorn, Wester Ross, Gordon Sangster, of Peterhead, would often have to interview candidates for temporary jobs.

One day, he heard a distinctive North-east voice outside his office, and in shambled a thin and nervous-seeming laddie who said he was looking for a job. "We were actually two men down at the time," Gordon wrote, "so this lad was a Godsend, but the rules of the firm were that I had to interview him formally. I more or less just went through the motions to keep the paperwork right."

Gordon started with a light-hearted question to try to calm the lad's nerves. He asked if the lad could make tea. The lad said he could.

"But can you drive a forklift?" Gordon asked.

The lad said: "It's surely an affa big teapot."

PETER KIDDIE used to run "a well-known fast-food outlet" in Aberdeen and was interviewing teenagers for four new positions. He asked one candidate if he had any experience in fast-food retail.

The youngster shook his head, then added: "Jist eatin it."

BILLY BREMNER (not the football player, as far as we know) described himself as a typical long-haired, grunting, teenage layabout in the Seventies. It was bad enough for his parents to have one such crea- ture in the house, according to Billy, but when his schoolmates, all cast from the same mould, visited every fourth Friday night, it became too much for his dad, Ian, who would sit there, determined not to yield his living-room, arms folded and sour of face.

One evening, the lads' discussion wore round to things they had known in their childhood, but which were no longer available in the Seventies.

"It was a real 'Div ye mind?' session," Billy wrote, "even though we were only 16 and 17. We must have sounded like pensioners: 'I mind Lucky Numbers caramels.' 'I mind liquorice straps.' 'I mind Fireball XL5.' 'I mind Champion, The Wonder Horse.'"

Then came a growl from the easy chair by the fireside: "And I mind fin freaks wis aa in circus tents."

TO DUFFTOWN in the late 1980s now, where 12- year-old Brian landed himself an unofficial weekend job sweeping a distillery yard and doing other odds and ends. It wasn't so much a job as a favour to Brian's dad, who also worked at the distillery and who wanted to get his son used to earning his own pocket money. Brian was promised 80p an hour.

When Brian's mum went along at lunchtime on the first Saturday to see if she could spy her son wielding his brush, she found him, instead, near to tears. When he spotted his mother, it all became too much for him and he began sobbing.

"Fit's adee?" she said.

"They said I'd get 80p an oor," he sobbed.

"Aye."

"Well, I've been here three oors and naebody's peyed me nithing."

COOKERY FAN Sandra Tait, of Montrose, went to the kirk jumble sale one Saturday morning and discovered a treasure trove of old cookery books. Her 13-year-old, Joshua, was helping her leaf through them when he came upon a particularly old example, well used, with congealed and crusty bits of food and mixture on most of its pages.

"Look, mum," Joshua said. "A cookbook with free samples."

A RETIRED Inverurie Academy teacher recalled starting her career in the 1950s and being determined that her classes would be more relaxed than was customary at the time. She was sure her pupils would achieve more if they didn't feel constantly under pressure.

On her first day with a fourth-year class, she began by explaining that although she wouldn't stand for any nonsense or indiscipline, she hoped that they would feel that she was approachable with any questions or problems, academic or personal, and that she would get to know them not just as pupils, but also as people.

Rolling up the map of Europe

At that, she turned to the blackboard. Alas, one of those maps, similar to window blinds on rollers, decided to roll itself up, the hook at its bottom catching on her skirt and lifting the skirt with it.

There was an appalled silence in the class as she struggled to regain her dignity, broken only by one lad at the back saying: "Well, we ken you better already."

DAIRY REP Sandy Cooper was plying his trade at Turriff one day and drove his van up a cul-de-sac bordering Markethill Primary School. Some of the pupils shouted and waved at him, so Sandy, being a cheery chap, waved back.

He sat writing for a minute or two, then got out and was greeted with a shout from behind the school fence of: "Hie, mister! Wid ye get oor ba back, please?"

"Nae bother," Sandy said, and he set off in the direction the lads were pointing out. At that moment, the school bell rang.

"Hurry, mister," came the panicky shout. "Hurry or we'll be late. Rin. Please hurry. Rin. Rin."

Then Sandy heard one voice say in mild disgust: "Ach, he's ower aul tae rin."

TO TORRY ACADEMY, Aberdeen, in the 1950s now, and a first-year class about to lose their teacher temporarily for maternity leave. Two small boys were deep in conversation about the teacher's obvious change in profile. Eventually, after daring each other to bring up the subject, one marched out to the front of the class.

"Miss, I ken fit's wrang wi you."

"Do you?"

"Aye, ye're pregnant."

"Is that so?"

"Aye, ye're haein a baby."

"Am I really? Well, well, well. Just you go back to your seat now and we'll carry on with the lesson."

As she turned to begin writing on the blackboard, she heard him sit down, lean across to his chum and say: "Did ye hear that? She's pregnant and she nivver even kent. I'd tae tell her."

A LIBRARIAN at one of the larger libraries in the North-east got in touch to say that she looked up from her desk one day to see standing in front of her one of the town bruisers. The lad, in his mid-teens, was not notably interested in books, so the librarian was surprised to see him, but delighted, too.

He mumbled that he had to complete a school exercise over the weekend and he needed a play by Shakespeare.

"Certainly," she said. "Which one?"

He looked at her, mystified, and said: "William."

A CELEBRATED Aberdeen architect, who will remain nameless, bought a summer-house in the Aboyne area in the 1930s, at roughly the same time as the famous Willing Shilling Fund was organising holidays in the countryside for poorer city children.

He recalled strolling round his grounds one summer day when he came upon a group of these boys staring up at a tall tree and having a terrific argument.

"Hie, mister," one of them shouted when they spotted him. "Fit's 'at things hingin up there?"

He walked up and explained that they were the especially large cones that blue-cedar trees always produced.

"See!" the inquisitor told his mates. "I telt ye they werna mealie poodins."

ONE TEACHER told us about receiving a sick note from a parent, explaining that her son had become ill after playing outside in bad weather while wearing trainers that were so old that the soles had been worn beyond repair. The note read: "Please excuse Alan from school. He has diarrhoea through a hole in his shoe."

RETIRED ENGLISH teacher Renee Falconer told us she once asked a second-year class to write a short essay entitled "What Poetry Means To Me."

One pupil wrote: "Poetry is when every line starts with a capital letter and doesn't reach the other side of the page."

Kissies and Bosies

North-east Man isn't given to overblown romantic gestures. Given the tales in this chapter, perhaps it's best kept that way.

GEORGE NOBLE, of Buckie, was sitting in his easy chair one night in the Sixties when his son, Alan, came home and announced he'd landed a plum role in the school play.

"Fit's 'at?" George inquired.

"He's the heid o the faimly; mairriet twenty-five year," Alan said.

"Stick in, loon," George said, going back to his paper. "Ye'll maybe get a spikkin pairt yet."

INVERURIE CLERKESS Ina Ellis remembers the mild conflict that arose between her parents every time the subject of her mother's best friend arose in conversation. "My mother adored her pal and my father couldn't stand the woman," Ina wrote.

"I must admit, she seemed to have an uncanny sense of timing and would always turn up at meal-times, thus making my mother feel obliged to invite her to stay and eat.

"My father stood it for so long until one evening, after he'd had a pretty rough day anyway, the pal turned up as usual, just as my mother was about to serve her home-made egg-and-bacon pie.

"'Oh, I div like hame cookin,' my mother's pal said.

"'In that case,' my dad said, 'bliddy weel bide at hame and cook.'"

THE PATH to romance wasn't easy for Donna Galbraith and Andy Patterin. Before they were married, Andy knew that Donna had a fantasy about being serenaded on Valentine's Night. For some reason that he still can't explain, Andy decided that not only would he serenade his beloved, he would do it nude.

That was risky, but his big mistake was to try a bit of Dutch courage at one of the town pubs. He rolled out at 9pm, staggering in the general direction of Donna's second-floor flat.

He disrobed quietly enough in the shadows behind a couple of front-garden bushes, but not even temperatures hovering at freezing point were enough to sober him up. He picked up a handful of gravel and flung it at the second-floor window.

When he saw the curtains pulling back, he threw his arms wide, displaying himself in all his shrivelled glory and began wailing over and over: "O, Sole Mio!"

Alas, Andy was still one street away from Donna's flat, and the elderly sisters who shared the flat were appalled and called the police 20 minutes later.

The bobbies had a hard time not laughing once Andy explained himself. Donna turned up to march him home. Andy has since confined his nude singing to the shower.

THE TABLOIDS worked themselves into a frenzy after Victoria Beckham announced that her son had been named Brooklyn because that was where he had been conceived. On the morning the news broke, two women on an Aberdeen bus were drawing the matter through hand when one observed: "In that case, my aulest should hiv been caaed Seaton Park."

INA AULD, of Bucksburn, was hearing from a neighbour that the neighbour's son had got himself engaged to a very tall girl from Dufftown.

"Tall?" Ina said.

"At least six fit," the neighbour said, at which the neighbour's husband added: "Aye, she could aet strae aff a reef."

INA ALSO recalls her days as a fairm quine in Buchan, and hearing two chiels in one of the village hotels on mart day, horsing into scotch broth and discussing their wives.

"There's nae a please in her aenoo," one said. "The least little thing I say or dee jist sets her aff."

"Ye're lucky," said the other. "Mine's a self-starter."

BACK TO the early 1930s now, when six-year-old Eric, from Donside, was asked by his auntie if he liked school. Eric said he did.

"It's a lang walk for ye," she said. "Twa mile there and twa mile back. Hiv ye naebody for company?"

"There's the quine up the road," Eric said, "bit I dinna like her."

"Fit's adee wi her?"

"She rins efter me and chases me and tries tae kiss me," Eric said.

Auntie laughed. "I widna worry aboot that, Eric," she said. "Jist you wait sivven–eicht year and it'll be a different story, mark ma words."

"I ken," Eric said. "I'll be able tae rin faister."

SOMEONE WHO signs himself just "Len" wanted us to know of his neighbours in Cattofield after the war. One evening, when the woman of the house was at home alone, there was a knock on the door. She went to the end of the lobby and cried: "Fit div ye wint?"

"Is this far Angus bides?"

"Aye," she sighed, sliding back the bolt, "jist cairry him in."

THE LATE Peter MacConnochie was a renowned pianist in Banffshire and West Aberdeenshire between the mid-1960s and the late 1970s. Although his favourite instrument was the church organ, Peter would also turn his hand to earning an extra fiver by playing piano at some of the classier wedding receptions in the two counties.

Peter sometimes had his doubts that some of his matrimonial clientele were as classy as they liked to pretend, and his favourite story came from one Banff wedding where he wasn't sure how well his somewhat up-market repertoire was being received by the guests.

Eventually, he took the microphone and asked for requests. There was a buzz of conversation followed by a portly gent, blurry of eye and unsteady of gait, shambling over to Peter, clapping a matey arm round his shoulder and slurring:

"Any requests?"

"Gie's some Picasso."

"FOO ARE YE gettin on wi the wife?"
"Jist great. We're nae spikkin."

FORMER BANFFSHIRE MP Hamish Watt remembered the tale of the farm being worked by three bachelor sons and where the kitchie deem had fallen pregnant.

The three lads' mother was horrified and shamed, and demanded to know of the parish doctor which of her sons he thought was the father.

"I dinna ken, Mary," the GP said, "bit there's ae thing for sure: ee're the grunnie."

WHEN MYLENE GRANT, of Ellon, went with her husband of 18 months to visit her mother at Peterhead, she thought she detected an atmosphere. When her husband left the room for a smoke, Mylene thought she would confront the situation head-on.

"Right. Fit's adee?" she asked.

"Am I never going to be a grandma?" blurted her mother.

Mylene started laughing. "Is that aa?" she said. "Well, we're nae rushin intae things, though we're keepin wir fingers crossed."

"Well," snapped her mother, "if that's fit ye're deein, ye've been misinformed."

ONE TORPHINS couple were celebrating their diamond wedding shortly after the last war and the village minister called and asked their secret for a long marriage.

"Well," said the husband, "on the day we got mairriet, I says tae Meg: 'Now, Meg, I've a gey sharp tongue in ma heid and you'll whiles get the roch edge o't, but fin ye've hid eneuch, jist you ging oot the door for a walk.'

"And she says tae me: 'I've a gey sharp tongue masel, so jist you dee the same.'"

"And that's wir secret: plenty fresh air and exercise."

TWO STONEHAVEN worthies were discussing modern loose morals, when one said proudly: "I had no idea if my wife was man or woman until I was married."

"Oh," said the other one, "I could hiv telt ye."

GARDENER BILLY DUGUID remembered visiting the home of a previous girlfriend at Banff in the 1970s and feeling a bit intimidated by how posh the girl's parents seemed to be.

"I managed to relax a bit," Billy wrote, "when the mother announced grandly: 'I hope you like goujons of sole. I prepared them myself. The recipe's Condom Blue.'"

AT A SMALL Banffshire village not a million miles from Aberlour, it became apparent that the extra-marital habits of a man of the parish were being discussed in great detail by the community.

At one evening event, the mostly female assembly

was dutifully appalled by such immorality. The phrase "his peer wife" cropped up several times.

The only man nearby, a brosey chiel in his sixties, was saying nothing. Soon, the women sought his views. "Wullie, fit decent man wid dee things like that? I mean, you wid nivver hiv slept wi anither man's wife, wid ye?"

"Nivver," Wullie said.

Then he took a swig of his shandy and grinned: "Dozed aff a coupla times, though."

The Shoppie

The shoppie, large or small, is often the focal point of a community, be it a village, parish or city district. Since all places where people gather are fountains of natural humour, we thought we'd devote a chapter to it once again.

SCHOOL COOK Alice Robertson was climbing the stairs to the popular Morgan McVeigh restaurant and tourist centre between Huntly and Inverurie when she had to stand aside for three women, one of them white-haired and elderly and the two others whom Alice took to be the woman's daughters.

One of the daughters said: "Did ye see they've got oatmeal soap?"

"Awa ye go," said the old lady. "Fa washes oatmeal?"

"DOUBLE SANDY" was the nickname of a celebrated Aberdeenshire chemist, otherwise known as Mr Alexander Alexander. Once, he had to reprimand a youth for smoking in his shop.

"Ye sell fags, though!" said the outraged teenager.

"Aye," said Sandy, "and I sell caster ile, tee."

SANDY STRONACH, Master of the Doric Festival, tells of an old woman returning, indignant, to a country shoppie between the wars with a box of matches that she had bought a few hours earlier.

"Yer spunks is weet," she chastised the grocer. "They winna crack."

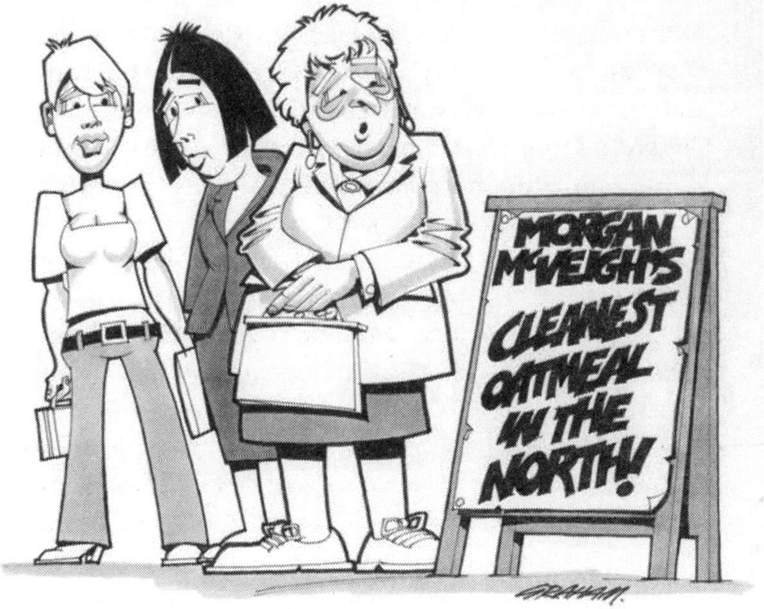
MORGAN McVEIGH'S
CLEANEST OATMEAL IN THE NORTH!
GRAHAM

The grocer demanded the box of matches, took one out, ran it across the backside of his moleskin trousers and it burst into flame first time.

"See?" he told her. "Nithin wrang wi them."

"Tyach," said the old woman. "I canna cairry your erse aboot wi me aa day."

IT SEEMS that Cuminestown once had one of those country emporia that stocked absolutely everything. One day, a farming chiel from the area turned up and asked: "Div ye stock cutlery?"

"We div that," said the owner.

"Grand," said the farmer. "Could I hae a chuntie?"

TEAROOMS ARE great places for meeting the North-east at first hand. Ann Young reported overhearing a conversation between two elderly women in the café of a well-known city store, which went something like:

"Did ye see *Taggart* last nicht?"

"Aye."

"Good, eh?"

"Aye."

"Did ye ken the murderer wis him?"

"Aye."

"Foo did ye ken? I didna ken."

"Weel, ye myn fin he wis in *Take The High Road* and his brither got jiled for killin the lassie?"

"Aye."

"There ye go. They're aa tarred wi the same brush, that faimly."

SANDY DUNCAN was a noted jeweller in the Rosemount area of Aberdeen for many years. People often popped in for a news, even when they had no need of jewellery or watch repairs, and Sandy encouraged them with friendly banter.

Occasionally, a customer could give as good as he got.

"Foo are ye gettin on wi that new watch I selt ye?" Sandy inquired of one customer one day.

"Jist gran," said the customer. "What a watch. It dis an oor in 55 minutes."

BANCHORY READER Mary Milne recalled an English gentleman visiting a country shop and asking the country quine who was behind the counter if she could recommend any places or nearby attractions that were worth visiting.

"Oh," said the girl, aware of the profound scenic and cultural limitations of her home parish. "Ye're best gaun oot aboot a bit."

Mary heard later that the tourist had been stopping people in the street and asking for directions to Ootabootabit.

A FAMOUS tale of an antiques shop on Deeside involves a customer buying six Victorian soup plates, but, just as they were being wrapped up, noticing a substantial crack along the bottom of one.

When this was pointed out, the assistant advised: "Ach, jist mak yer soup a bittie thicker."

SANDY REID used to run a corner shoppie in Cotton

Street, Aberdeen, and found it difficult to keep his store stocked with all the faddy products that dieting women wanted. When the banana diet came along, he was delighted, because he knew that keeping stock would be simple.

One customer on the diet was Jean, an ample matron whose husband worked in the shipyards. Jean had tried every diet from every magazine, but with little success. Then she started the banana diet and adapted it after a few weeks, on the advice of another women's magazine, to include peanuts (for protein) and palm oil (for light fats).

When Jean hadn't turned up in the shop for a few days, Sandy stopped her husband as he was buying his morning packet of cigarettes before heading off to the shipyards. Was the bananas, peanuts and palm-oil diet doing Jean any good?

"Hisna deen nithing for her ata," said Jean's man, "though ye should see her climmin trees."

SANDY ALSO started stocking a new ice-cream supply, hoping to please his customers with a new home-made taste, but the conservative ice-cream aficionados of Cotton Street and round about were suspicious of new products.

One shipyard worker turned up at lunchtime and saw the new display. "Is yer ice-cream pure?" he demanded.

"As pure as the lass o yer dreams," Sandy replied.

"In that case," said the customer, "gie's twenty fags."

FARMER JIMMY SIMPSON, of Huntly, told us of the old-style country emporium, where the grocer was proud of his comprehensive stock of fine malt whiskies.

"I've got the lachin kind, the greetin kind, the freenly kind, the fechtin kind, the singin kind and the dour kind," the grocer used to say.

"The funny thing is, they aa come oot o the same bottle."

FLORIST MARY JESSIMAN prided herself on helping even her most nervy customers find exactly the arrangement they wanted. When one elderly chap turned up in her Aberdeen shop one Wednesday afternoon, she jaloused straight away that he wasn't comfortable being in a florist's shop, and she decided that he needed help.

"The wife and me hisna been spikkin," he said. "It's as weel that I buy her flooers and get it oot o the road. And wid it be possible for ye say on the card: 'You were right after all.'?"

Mary smiled and said she was sure that would be possible. "How much were you thinking of spending?" she said. "Twenty pounds . . . 30 . . . 35?"

The man blanched. "I wis thinkin mair 10 or 12," he said. "She wisna *that* richt."

THOSE OF you who, like the two of us, manage a wee quiet cheer every time you hear somebody pittin on the pan-loaf and promptly faain doon throwe't will enjoy this tale from a Keith quine who visited one of Aberdeen's posher stores (now defunct) some years ago.

The store's assistants were noted for doing their best to match, even exceed, what they imagined were the social standing and graces of their extremely airchie clientele.

One such assistant was caught unawares by a blue-rinsed customer waiting patiently at the counter for service. The assistant bustled across, smoothed down her outfit and said: "Good morning, moddom, and fit wye may I help you?"

OVERHEARD IN the queue at Summerhill Post Office, Aberdeen: "Isn't it a richt peety aboot Tony Blair and his wife?"

"Fit wye?"

"Him wi sae muckle teeth and her wi hardly ony."

THE LONG-TIME grocer at Dunecht, Basil Lessel, could stand many things and many people, but he couldn't thole grocery reps, who were the bane of his extremely busy shop life.

According to Jimmy Sim, of Culter, Basil used to be visited by so many reps that he couldn't get on with running his shop. Basil finally snapped when one such cocky young rep arrived from Aberdeen thinking he would try the bright-and-breezy approach to win some custom from Basil.

"Lovely morning, Mr Lessel," he said.

Basil replied drily: "Did ye come aa the wye fae Aiberdeen tae tell me that?"

ANOTHER COUNTRY shopkeeper – let's just say somewhere in mid-Buchan – was known everywhere from Fraserburgh to Ellon as a man for whom every penny was a prisoner, and who would no more offer a bargain or money off than he would cut off his own hands.

One of his customers said of him drily one day: "He's that ticht that fin he bends his knees, his een close."

FROM INVERURIE now, and Betty Forbes told us her mother had returned from doing her messages in the Safeway supermarket on the edge of town. Her mum was excited and flustered all at once.

"His something happened, mither?" Betty asked.

"The mannie in front o me in the queue at the checkoot collapsed," said Betty's mother. "Ae minute he wis jist stannin there, shovin his tatties up the line, the next minute . . . BOOF! . . . flat oot."

"Was he all right?" Betty asked.

"Dinna ken. Fin I left, they were still giein him artificial insemination."

Doon on the Fairm

Agricultural humour is the backbone of the North-east. As, indeed, is agriculture.

BACK IN the 1980s, when it was fashionable among farmers in England to sell up and move to the northern half of Scotland, thereby doubling or trebling their acreage, Peter and Patricia Richardson moved to a smallholding just outside Keith.

Keen to make themselves known in the community, they visited one of the town bars and were soon getting on famously with the locals.

"And hiv ye been bothered wi the moth?" one of the worthies inquired presently.

Peter and Pat looked at each other. "The moth?"

"Aye, ye hinna been bothered yet?"

"Not that we know of," said Peter. "Should we be worried?"

The worthy turned to address the bar: "They hinna hid the moth yet, boys." And a roar of approval got up.

Peter and Pat were beginning to grow a little unsettled, for their croft was out of the way and no one had warned them of possible infestations and crop damage. No amount of pleading would make the bar customers spill the secret, and the Richardsons went home more than a little anxious.

They were just making themselves a late-night cup of tea when there was a knock at the door. Pat looked at the clock. It wasn't far short of midnight; they were half a mile from the nearest neighbour, and it was pitch-black outside.

Both went to the back door, and there, on the step, stood Wullie, a well-known drouth in the area, unsteady on his feet and obviously looking for more drink now that the pubs had closed.

"Aye," he said. "I saw yer licht on."

They had finally met The Moth.

BACK TO the Saturday-night dances that were popular at wee country halls throughout the North-east between the wars. At one time, the "Mississippi Dip" was a fashionable dance, involving both parties hesitating, then bending the knees slightly as if about to drop into a crouching position.

At Cushnie Hall, one farmer invited a young lass who was new to the area up to the floor. She had never danced this dance before and, as the band struck up, inquired nervously: "Excuse me, bit fan exactly div ye dip?"

"Weel," the farmer said, "usually the back eyn o the season."

A STRICHEN farmer reported stopping one of his pals in the street and inquiring: "Wis that you that gaed doon by on a bike the ither nicht and waved?"

"It wis," the second man said, before pausing and adding: "If it hidna been me, I widna hiv waved."

SOME OF the loneliest farming spots in the North-east were the Cabrach crofts. One day, a group of tourists happened past on their way from Donside

The "Mississippi Dip"

to Dufftown, and paused at the top of the glen to drink in the view of all the rolling moorland.

A crofter was nearby mending fences, and the tourists strolled over and complimented him on his homeland, adding: "You're very lucky to stay in such a lovely spot."

"That may be so," he told them. "Bit foo wid you like tae hae tae traivel 15 mile ilky time ye wintit a dram?"

"Well why don't you buy half a dozen bottles and keep them in the house?" suggested one of the tourists.

"Na," said the crofter. "Whisky disna keep."

ONE OF the North-east's most celebrated stock-brokers from the 1940s was Hugh Park, who used to tell of attending Maud Mart with a cattle-dealer friend and watching a farmer standing beside a pen of 20 steers waiting to go into the ring.

The dealer approached the farmer and, after checking that the beasts were his, asked how much he was expecting for them.

The farmer named a price, and the dealer, who was anxious to conclude a sale and get back to Glasgow quickly, offered £2 a head more than the asking price, hoping that would be sweetener enough.

The farmer accepted, then went quiet.

The dealer asked if the price was all right and the farmer replied: "I wyte it's aaricht, bit I'd hiv likit a lot mair spikkin aboot it."

HUGH WAS sitting in the bar of the Royal Athenaeum in Aberdeen, which will be remembered by older readers as "Jimmie Hay's", after a long-lost former owner, when another Buchan client and farmer arrived.

Hugh asked what the farmer would like to drink. "Na, na, Hugh," came the reply. "I'm nae drinkin the day. I'll jist hae a whisky."

HUGH WAS trapped in the 1947 snowdrift that paralysed much of Buchan, but he managed to find lodgings at a small farm. As the evening wore on, he became more and more puzzled by how such a poor and small farm could survive. Before he left the next day, he asked the farmer.

"Weel," said the farmer, pointing at the solitary farmhand. "He works for me, bit I canna pey him, so in twa year he gets the fairm. Then I work for him till I get it back."

COLONEL JACK REID, of Cromleybank, Ellon, had a famous pedigree herd of beef shorthorns and occasionally let a smaller-scale farmer nearby in Formartine, who had two shorthorn cows, have the use of a bull for free.

One of these cows produced a good bull calf, which the farmer did not have castrated and kept on for breeding. Colonel Jack was at the old Ellon Mart one day and overheard the bull's proud owner talking to a potential client for the use of the young animal.

"Is't a good stock-getter?" the potential client inquired.

"Guaranteed, min," said the owner. "Better than that, he'll sen' yer heifers hame wi smiles on their faces."

DURING THE surge of union activity of the 1930s, a union official was dispatched round Buchan to see if he could drum up membership among farm workers.

He came to a small place near Maud and asked to speak to the farmer. The farmer appeared at the byre door and the union official explained his mission. "How many folk have you working here?" he inquired.

"Twa men and an eediot," the farmer said.

"And how much do the men get paid?"

"Thirty bob a week."

"Fair enough. And what about the idiot?"

"He gets new dungars and new beets fin he needs them, and he gets his keep."

The union official shook his head. "No, no, no," he said. "That's exploitation of the working classes. We canna hae that. I'm needin tae spik tae him."

"Weel," the farmer said. "Ye *are* spikkin tae him."

IN THE late 1940s, Tarland WRI asked one of the male villagers if he would organise a men's night, at which the women of the Howe of Cromar would be entertained by the local fellows doing their best musically, vocally, humorously or in whatever other way occurred to them.

One was a young English agricultural student, Mike Howden, who was on a placement at a nearby training farm.

Halfway through the programme, a trio sporting a melodeon, a moothie and a fiddle strode onstage. Suddenly, the MC realised that there were no seats for the trio and shouted a request: "Quick! Three cheirs for the band!"

At which point, the unwitting young Mr Howden began calling: "Hip-hip, hooray! Hip-hip . . ."

GEORGE SMITH was a bank agent at Turriff and one day an old customer, a Mr Kindness who had a croft at Auchterless, turned up to do some financial business.

During the proceedings, George asked Mr Kindness: "Did ye nivver think o gettin mairriet?"

"Weel," said Mr Kindness. "It's like this: an aul een's nae eese and a young een winna hae me."

FORWARD TO 1978 now, when a young family had just moved to the Chapel of Garioch area and were struggling to understand the broad Doric of their neighbours. "It was bad enough for me," the mother told us, "but I hadn't realised how much the children were struggling, too."

The youngsters, aged eight and four, were intrigued one day when a farming neighbour offered to bring along her pony to let the children see. As expected, the children were delighted. Seeing their enchantment, the neighbour urged them: "On ye go, noo. Dinna be feart. Gie the pony a clappie."

At which point the two stood back and shyly offered the animal a round of applause.

Characters

It's often said that Scotland doesn't have any characters any more. That's nonsense. There are still plenty of characters; we just don't recognise them yet. As one of our correspondents told us: "When he's alive, he's a pest, a nuisance or a show-off. It's only when he's deid that he becomes a character."

ONE OF the legends of the North-east motor trade was Jackie Urquhart, who plied his business in upwards of 30 different showrooms from the 1940s to the 1970s everywhere from Elgin to Peterhead to Stonehaven.

It was his habit of moving to a new employer almost every year, it seemed, that earned him his nickname, in the trade, of "Hit-the-Road Jack".

Like all good salesmen, Jackie enjoyed the cut and thrust of closing the deal, and was often disappointed if the customer capitulated too early, for he liked sweetening the pill with little extras that were supposedly free, but whose price had already been built into the cost of the car.

His favourite of many car-trade stories concerned the early 1970s, when metallic paint began to arrive. It was regarded as the utmost in good taste and high automotive fashion, although it added roughly 5% to the price of a car. Jackie, however, saw "the paint" as the ultimate bargaining tool.

His customers on the occasion in question were an elderly husband and wife from the country, who sat patiently listening to Jackie's patter and playing their cards close by saying nothing.

When even Jackie began to sweat at the unusually deadpan response, he flung his hands back in the gesture of capitulation so beloved of old hams and said: "OK. OK. You've got me. If you sign up now, I'll throw in the paint for nothing."

It was the first time the customers had showed signs of animation. "Ye better throw in the pent," the man said. "We're nae for a car that's nae pentit."

JACKIE ALSO shared a car salesman's cynicism for all his non-salesmen colleagues. As far as Jackie was concerned, everyone from the suits in the boardroom to the mechanics in the service bay conspired against the sales force.

One of his favourite approaches to new members of the sales team was to introduce himself and say: "D'ye ken fit's the motor trade's guaranteed wye tae avoid catchin a caul?"

"No."

"Gie't a parts number. Then naebody gets it."

WHEN JACKIE'S son, Ewen, announced he wanted to become a mechanic, it took a while for Jackie to adjust to the idea. Then, according to Ewen, he took the boy aside and said: "Div you ken the first thing aboot bein a car mechanic?"

Ewen said: "Well . . ."

"Well," Jackie said, "the first thing tae ken is foo tae open the bonnet, stand back, rub yer chin, shak her heid and say: 'This'll be pricey.'"

"I'll throw in the paint for nothing."

A FYVIE reader recalled a guard on the old Turriff train before the war who had a notoriously bad memory, and who would frequently forget which station they were at. Stumped for an announcement that allowed him to work round his lapse of memory, he would walk through the length of the train calling: "Here ye are for far ye're gaun. Aa you in here for oot there, get aff."

ANOTHER CELEBRATED character in the motor trade was Henry Leask, of Cheyne's Motorcycles, who used to travel daily to work on the old subbie train from Culter to Aberdeen.

One morning, an old body sporting wrinkly stockings, curlers under her turban, dilapidated specs and laden with message bags peched her way into Henry's first-class compartment and plunked herself down in the seat opposite. She gave Henry a friendly, but toothless, grin.

Henry was a gentleman of the old school. He didn't mind any companion, but he thought her an unlikely first-class traveller and feared that she might be embarrassed when the ticket-collector arrived. He leaned forward and said, in a discreet whisper: "Excuse me, my dear, but you're in a first-class seat."

She beamed, and replied loudly: "I ken that fine, loon, bit it's ma birthday the day and I'm giein my dowp a treat."

TIMMER ROGERS sold bags of firewood from an old dray cart pulled by an even older horse before

World War I. One day, the horse finally collapsed and died in a clatter of harness, shafts and chains.

Residents and passers-by rushed to see what all the commotion was about and found Timmer looking down sadly at the lifeless remains of his faithful old servant.

After a few moments, he turned to an onlooker and, with a tear in his eye, said: "I've nivver seen it deein that afore."

A FAMOUS tale about post-war building magnate Willie Logan involved Willie going on a site visit to the Tay Road Bridge in 1965 and spotting one of his workmen with the sole of his workboot flapping away from the uppers.

"What do you think you're playing at?" he demanded. "Don't you know that's not safe on a building site?"

"I ken, Mr Logan," the hapless labourer said, "bit I dinna get paid till Friday and I canna afford tae hae the beets repaired or buy a new pair."

Willie reached into his jacket pocket and pulled out the most monstrous bundle of £20 notes, all kept together by an elastic band, that the young labourer had seen. The lad's eyes widened and smile brightened – but not for long.

"Here," Willie said to him, and he pulled off the elastic band and handed it over. "That'll stop the flapping until Friday."

THE LATE David Welch, Director of Links and Parks in Aberdeen, was the man widely credited with

Aberdeen's record number of wins in the annual "Britain in Bloom" competition. He was also a fine and witty after-dinner speaker, and a man with a kindly touch as far as the city was concerned.

David was touring one of the city parks one day and came across one of the older corporation gardeners, who was immensely proud of the grass that he looked after. He was so proud that he had erected home-made signs warning visitors that they should not sit, stand or walk on such lush pasture.

When David asked who had put the signs there, the gardener said defiantly that *he* had. David looked round at the children playing in the park, in the way that public parks are meant to be used by the public, and said gently to his employee: "I don't think it'll work."

"Fit wye nae?"

David pointed out two small boys playing Cowboys and Indians. "Because," he said, "an Indian being chased for his life by a cowboy hasn't the time to stop and look at your signs."

JOURNALIST ROBERT URQUHART, who came from Buchan and who made his name on *The Scotsman*, had a sister whose fine singing voice meant that she was in great demand for concerts throughout Aberdeenshire.

At one such concert in a small Buchan village, Robert's sister was giving a hand with the washing-up in the hall kitchen when in came Jimmy, who, in the vernacular of the day, "hid a bit o a wint". In other words, Jimmy wasn't all there.

The front door of the little wooden hall was on the road, but the ground dropped away steeply behind to a track with steps leading down to it. After his tea and cakes, Jimmy disappeared outside. Presently, there came several loud thumps and yelps.

"Mercy," Robert's sister said, "what's that noise?"

"Ach," said one of the village women. "Dinna fash. That'll be Jimmy coontin the steps wi his heid."

THE LATE Sandy Mutch, long-time councillor and, latterly, Convener of Grampian Regional Council, used to tell of finding the archetypal absent-minded professor at the world-famous Rowett Research Institute, just outside Aberdeen.

The scientist had a hand-written badge pinned to his lapel, reading:

DO NOT GIVE ME A LIFT HOME
I HAVE THE CAR TODAY

KINCARDINE READERS will have heard of "Kirkie Davie", the late David Milne who once farmed Kirktown of Fetteresso and who latterly owned the Mill o Forest Dairy at Stonehaven and rose to be a baillie on the town council.

Davie's command of bad language was legendary. One mart Thursday, he was in The Square at Stonehaven with a few cronies when Miss Ramsay, a very prim and proper teacher, passed on her way home for lunch.

Approaching the group, she remonstrated: "Oh, Mr Milne. That's terrible language you're using, and with children passing on their way home from school."

Davie turned to his cronies and demanded: "Right. Fitna een o you buggers is sweirin?"

ON ANOTHER occasion, while Kirkie Davie was sitting on the bench as baillie, a farm servant appeared before him on a charge of being drunk and using obscene language in public.

Davie fined him 15/- and added: "One thing I winna tolerate is this bliddy bad language."

WE'LL STEP up several social gears now for a story involving Queen Victoria ("Yer Mujesty"). The North-east's most celebrated home-economics expert, Muriel Clark, of Aboyne, remembered, in one of her books, that Victoria liked to visit the Balmoral estate workers, often at short notice and often at meal-times.

On one such visit, Victoria was especially taken with the fine smells from the cauldron of Scotch Broth that was bubbling merrily on the black-lead range. She inquired as to the ingredients.

"Weel, ma'am," the woman of the house said, "there's barley intill't, there's pizz intill't, there's carrots intill't . . ."

"Yes, yes, yes," cried the monarch, "barley, peas and carrots, but where do you get this 'intill't'?"

TWO BROTHERS – let's call them Davie and Wullie – worked a croft near a small village north of Deeside before the last war, and Davie was partial to a dram on a Saturday night. When lousin time came, Davie would give himself a dicht here and there, then board his ancient BSA motorcycle and hotter his way into the village to weet his thrapple.

With no breathalysers to impede festivities, Davie would make the most of his night off and, by closing time, was generally past caring. One Saturday night, he had teetered out to his BSA, fired her up, pointed her in the right direction and set off for home.

Alas, while attempting to round a sharp bend, Davie went one way and the bike went the other. Three lads following a few minutes later in a car chanced upon the scene, and while one went to haul the BSA out of the ditch, another went to dust down Davie and be sure that he was none the worse for his mischanter.

As the rescuer got Davie on his feet and was brushing him down, he exclaimed: "Michty, Davie, ye've rippit a hole in the erse o yer brikks."

"No," Davie said. "I hinna."

Yet the flapping material and large aperture was there for all to see. "I wyte ye hiv," said the rescuer. "There ye go: a great muckle hole. See?"

"No, I hinna," Davie said, swaying gently. "They're Wullie's brikks."

TO INVERBERVIE in the early 1930s now, and Edward Milne, an employee of the North of Scotland Bank in the town has just got married.

James Gibb, of Hallgreen Castle, on his first subsequent visit to the bank made no comment on Edward's recent nuptials, but then, as he was about to leave, turned and said: "Aye, Mr Milne, yer penny pies'll cost ye tippence noo."

STILL AT Inverbervie, older Kincardine residents will remember William Lyon, the businessman and town provost. One day in the bank, one of his contemporaries, a not-so-successful businessman, came in.

They got into conversation, when the poorer of the two said: "Aye, Mr Lyon, bit money's nae aathing."

"Maybe no," Mr Lyon replied, "bit a poun in yer pooch is affa handy fin ye wint tae rin an eeran."

The Toon

What would life in North-east Scotland be without the friendly rivalry between city and country, Teuchter and Toonser? Although we're both proud sons of the country, we still think that the Granite City deserves a chapter of its own.

A PARTY of English visitors was installed at the Prince of Wales hostelry and public house in the centre of Aberdeen when the subject got round to the supposed meanness of Aberdonians.

One who fancied himself as a bit of a wag leaned over to local man Ackie Sangster at the next table and said: "Do you know the difference between an Aberdonian and a coconut?'

"No," Ackie said.

"You can get a drink out of a coconut," the wag said, to roars of laughter from his compatriots.

Ackie had the good grace to manage a smile and, when the laughter had died down, made to dip into his pocket for change: "Wid you lads like a drink then?" he said.

"That's very decent of you," said the Englishman. "We could all do with a drink, thank you."

"Fine," Ackie said. "Awa and buy a coconut."

TO APPRECIATE the next tale, you have to understand, as all self-respecting Aberdonians have done for decades, that Aitken's Bakery is one of the prime purveyors of North-east patisserie and boulangerie.

Taxi-driver Norman Duncan found himself in a

soirée in one of Aberdeen's pubs when the topic of conversation got round to dieting. Mr Duncan, who wishes it to be known that he is actually a very healthy eater, kept his counsel as his companions explored the various merits of the grapefruit diet, the vitamin B diet and seemingly every other faddy diet humankind had invented.

"Fit aboot you, Nommie?" one of his chums asked presently. "Are you an Atkins Diet man?"

"No," Nommie said. "I'm mair the Aitken's Diet."

"Aitken's Diet?" said the group.

"Aye," Nommie said. "Ivry mornin, four rowies and half a dizzen cream buns."

IN A SIMILAR vein, one Aberdeen secretary wrote to tell us that her boss's idea of a balanced diet was a pint in each hand.

BUS-DRIVER Ian Anderson was on duty the day that Aberdeen introduced the exact-change system on its corporation fleet. Ian stopped near Holburn Junction, where one of his regular clients, an older woman from Great Western Road, handed him a pound note.

"Sorry," Ian said. "Exact change only."

"Laddie," said the woman, "I'll gie ye exact change fin you tak me exactly far I'm wintin tae ging."

THE GRAMPIAN Industrialist of the Year crown for 2001 was bestowed on Alasdair Locke, of the Abbot Group, a successful concern which has fingers in many energy-related pies, but is noted particularly as a leading maker of alternative-energy generating equipment.

"I'm mair the Aitken's Diet"

Perhaps that explains Alasdair being hailed by the awards-dinner MC as: "Our winner for 2001, Alasdair Locke, the second-biggest generator of wind in the UK."

PRIDE IN your Aberdonian heritage starts young. Helen Fraser, of Cults, bade farewell to her five-year-old grandson when he and his family left to start a new life in North Uist. His first taste of school involved the teacher asking him and his classmates to take a piece of paper each and write the digit "1" several times.

Task completed, they queued up to show teacher their handiwork. While waiting patiently, our exiled Aberdonian noticed, with mounting alarm, that almost all of the 1s that the other children had drawn were different from his.

While he had crafted digits with a slope and a little serif line at the bottom, on which each 1 stood, his new classmates had all drawn simply a series of short vertical lines.

When he reached the front of the queue, he handed his teacher the paper and, before she had time to say anything, announced: "These are *Aberdeen* ones. And, anyway, I'm brand new around here."

BACK IN 1987, NorthSound Radio in Aberdeen ran a summer series aiming to put people back in touch with long-lost relatives and friends. To kick off the series, the station aired a studio discussion and phone-in, intending to trawl over successful stories, and hoping to dig up a few touching tales of reunion or loss at the same time.

When the presenter asked listeners for their tips on how best to go about locating long-lost Northeast family members, 17 callers phoned to advise: "Say you've won the Lottery."

DRAUGHTSMAN ANDY McKIM was going through security at Aberdeen Airport when the man in front of him was hauled out of the line for a random search. The chap wasn't best pleased and took it as a great personal affront.

As the security officer patted him down and ran the metal-detector over him, the man was almost beside himself with frustration, resentment and fury. The security man soon picked up this wee atmosphere that was building and said: "It's all right, sir. Please be patient. It's a random check. Just the luck of the draw."

"Just the luck of the draw?!" spluttered the man. "Just the luck of the draw?! In that case, come and fill out my !@£$%! Lottery ticket on Saturday!"

RECRUITMENT CONSULTANT Jim Petrie specialises in finding executive personnel for the oil industry. One question on his application form is: "In which areas of the world would you NOT be prepared to work?"

One applicant filled in: "Libya and Glasgow. (Libya negotiable.)"

IS THERE anyone as bitchy as someone who has fallen out with a neighbour? Ethel Baird, of Kincorth, Aberdeen, recalls having to live between two feuding neighbours during the Sixties. They had once been the best of pals, but had fallen out over something trivial, and went to their graves still not having made up.

"The exchange I remember," Ethel wrote, "Was when the neighbour on my left made a great show of striding down her garden path one summer evening, heading for a taxi and, presumably, a night on the town. She liked to dress up for an evening out and was prone to very elaborate hairdos.

"The other neighbour was visiting me at the time and we were both standing at the window watching from behind the net screens, which the dressed-up neighbour must have known perfectly well or she wouldn't have been putting on such a show.

"Anyway, by way of conversation, I noted the very elaborate hairdo and said: 'Some time I'll hae tae ask her foo lang it taks tae dee her hair.'"

The foe replied: "She disna ken, Ethel. She's nivver there."

IF YOU don't have a good command of the Doric, this next tale will mean nothing to you, but it tickles the rest of us. Indeed, the struggle non-Doric speakers have in appreciating that the dialect isn't just slang English is illustrated well by this tale from Cults, Aberdeen, where an English family arrived at the height of the oil boom, only to discover that their new granite villa had an infestation of wasps, or some such, in the roof space.

One of the woman's new neighbours gave her the name of an old country gent from the Bieldside area who was reputed to have a way with pest control.

He listened patiently to the symptoms and then demanded: "Hiv ye a bike?"

"Pardon?" she said.

"Hiv ye a bike?" he repeated.

"Well, yes," she said, "though it hasn't been used for years and I think the tyres are flat."

WHEN IAN ANDERSON was a young accountant in Aberdeen, he was dispatched for a week every quarter to do business out of a hotel room in Lerwick. This involved travelling on the Shetland ferry, which, as regular users will know, has always been liable to rough seas.

Ian was the worse for one such trip and, sitting beside an elderly chap out on the deck and holding his heaving stomach, noted that the man appeared to be unperturbed by the rough weather. "What's the best thing for seasickness?" Ian asked.

"Whisky," the man said.

"Dis that stop it?" Ian asked.

"No," the man said, "bit ye taste it gaun doon and ye get tae taste it comin back up again."

TWO PENSIONERS who were leaving Aberdeen Airport after returning home from holiday bumped into an acquaintance who was waiting to collect someone from another flight. Our source, one of the airport policemen, told us the ensuing conversation went as follows:

"Hiv ye been awa?"

"Aye, Fuerteventura."

"Fuerteventura? Far's that?"

"Dinna ken. We jist got aff the plane and there it wis."

SHORTLY AFTER a circus had visited the Links in the summer of 1934, the minister at nearby St Clements Church discovered that a dead donkey had been laid at the back door of his church; apparently this was a custom among travelling folk of the time to ensure that their animals were given a Christian send-off.

The minister phoned the Town House to arrange to have the animal taken away, but the clerk, either assuming it was a joke or being genuinely unhelpful, said: "I'm sorry, but I thought it was the duty of ministers to bury the dead."

"It is," said the minister, "but I thought I'd better inform the next of kin first."

ONE OF the most celebrated characters in Aberdeen between the wars was "Sojer", a man whom life had treated rather harshly, who had no fixed abode, and who spent his days marching up and down Union Street, King Street and round the Castlegate and the harbour as if he was on a parade ground.

Most of the shopkeepers kept a kindly eye out for "Sojer", and, one winter, when it became clear that he was suffering badly with a hacking cough, called out a doctor to attend to him.

The doctor offered the treatment free of charge: a bottle of pills with the instruction to take one three times a day after meals.

"Very good, sir," said "Sojer", saluting. "And far div I get the meals?"

The Papers

Journalism is a source of robust humour, especially the local press that publishes and sells throughout northern Scotland. Here are some of the cleaner tales that we were told.

WHEN ANNIE ROSS was a young woman-about-town in Aberdeen before moving to Derbyshire, she would often find herself bustling up Union Street, at busy times, where the newspaper vendors would be in full song.

On one particularly busy afternoon, she found her attention attracted by the billboards on all sides of a vendor's box, so she slowed as she passed.

"Evenin Express!" called the vendor at full volume. "City la-test!"

Annie's attention was now caught by the bill, so she began squinting at the copies of the paper laid on top of the vendor's box to see if she could glean a few more details.

"Evenin Express!" cried the vendor. "City la-tesssssst!"

She took a step forward and kinked her head round so she wouldn't be reading upside down, and that was when she heard the vendor shout:

"Evenin Express! Hire-purchase terms are available!"

WHEN JIM DOLAN was chief football writer on *The Press and Journal*, he was obliged to travel round the country attending Premier League matches,

"Hire-purchase terms are available!"

to follow Scottish teams on their European ventures, and to cover the Scotland team in internationals.

On one such occasion in the Central Belt, Jim found himself in the back of a cab, and the chatty cabbie asked him what was his line of work. Jim explained.

"Really?" said the cabbie, fascinated. "I wis a fitba player masel in ma young day."

"Is that so?" Jim said. "Who did you play for?"

"Cowdenbeath. Then I wis transferred tae East Stirlin. And ye ken how much ma transfer fee wis?"

"No."

"Nithin."

There was a silence in the cab for a few moments, then the cabbie added: "And that wis a lotta money in them days."

THE LOCAL-GOVERNMENT correspondent of *The Press and Journal* throughout the 1970s and 1980s was Gordon Mackay, who used to tell of one his colleagues being out golfing one morning and slicing his ball into the rough. Being an Aberdonian, the colleague spent a good half-hour searching for it, unaware that his every move was being watched by an old woman.

Eventually, he spotted her and she beckoned him over.

"I've been watchin ye lookin for yer ba," she said. "I didna wint tae bother ye, bit wid it be cheatin if I telt ye far it is?"

RON KNOX, former Assistant Editor of *The Press*

and Journal, was attending a professional dinner at the Beach Ballroom, Aberdeen, in the early 1990s when he spotted the maitre d'hotel, sporting a clipboard and a concerned look, walking round the tables.

He leaned down to whisper to a woman seated two places away from Ron. "Excuse me, madam. Are you a vegan?"

"No," she said. "Aquarius."

IT'S NOT just the red-top tabloids that can create clever wordplay in their headlines. *The Press and Journal* ran a tale in 1983 about a Glasgow tour operator who fleeced thousands of customers with promises of cut-price safaris and cruises, then scarpered with the deposits.

The *Press and Journal* heading was: Tour Allure a Lie.

BACK IN the days when the North Sea oil industry was a hive of activity and young businesses were making huge fortunes, *The Press and Journal* carried a recruitment advertisement from a contract cleaning company looking desperately for a manager.

In case prospective applicants were being put off by the worry that they would be expected to don the Marigolds and wield the Vim themselves, the ad-agency copy included the reassuring line that the "successful applicant would be mainly managing the business and not cleaning himself".

THE UNCLE of one of our contacts was an insurance agent in Aberdeen and used to collect premiums by going door-to-door in the evenings. At one such home, the man of the house opened the door.

Once inside, the insurance agent, somewhat tired, it must be said, inquired: "And how's your wife keeping? Is she still? . . ."

Something in the householder's reaction made the insurance man pause, prompting our man to recall that the wife's death notice had appeared in the columns of *The Press and Journal* a few weeks previously.

Anxious to make amends without being clumsy, he made the mistake of ploughing on: "Is she still . . . dead?"

WHEN RUSSELL REID retired as Editor of *The Sunday Post* in 2001, he regaled colleagues with tales from his 44 years in journalism, including an experience sitting on the press bench during a case at Arbroath Burgh Court in the late 1950s.

The chairman of the bench was one of the town bakers, and the case involved a woman who had just been found guilty of some misdemeanour or other.

The baker leaned imperiously towards the dock and said: "Has the accused anything to say before I pass sentence?"

The wifie squared her jaw and said: "Aye. Stop ma rolls."

FORMER WRITER and sub-editor for the *Evening Express* Joan Elrick moved later to Upper Deeside and heard the legend of a commercial traveller visiting the area and needing to find a particular crofter somewhere between Braemar and Ballater.

Having located the croft in question, he found that the man of the house was not in; it was the man's wife who came to the door.

"Aye, he's aboot somewye," she advised the traveller. "He's likely doon seein tae the pigs. Awa doon ye go. Ye'll easy ken him. He's weerin a hat."

THE PRESSURE of turning out a daily paper is the only excuse for the following famous blooper from *The Press and Journal* in the early 1970s. The feature told of a Banchory teenager landing a plum summer job with the London Symphony Orchestra. The feature explained:

"It is Noreen's job to check over the musicians' parts before each performance."

NOW FOR a classified advertisement from the *Evening Express* in the early 1980s, which we suspect was placed as a joke:

FOR SALE
Pure-bred Doberman guard dog.
Guaranteed fierce.
Contact the Trauma Unit
Dr Gray's Hospital, Elgin.

AND HERE'S one from the *Turriff Advertiser* in the mid-1970s, when a drapery store in the town was advertising a clearance sale of old stock that had been in storage in the loft for so long that most of the items would have needed a wash and an airing before they could be worn.

Part of the consignment was a range of outdated

men's underwear, which perhaps explained the following line in the advertisement:

MEN'S LONG JOHNS (SLIGHTLY SOILED)

No word as to how sales went.

THE AGRICULTURAL EDITOR of *The Press and Journal*, Joe Watson, remembers a well-known North-east farmer buying a substantial acreage in Estonia, shortly after that country devolved from the USSR in the 1990s. Keen students of farming will know that the rich Baltic farmland was going for virtual pennies an acre, and was too good a prospect for UK farmers to ignore.

Wanting a new manager for his new place, the farmer did the obvious thing and advertised in *The Press and Journal*. He had many replies, but the strangest of all was a phone call from a Keith direction.

"Fit exactly is there on this fairm?" inquired the applicant.

The farmer told him of the many acres of arable ground, the large dairy herd, the seed-potato speciality and the small piggery. There was also a considerable number of staff who would need quite a bit of management to be brought up to Western standards of farm practice.

"Maist fairm loons need 'at," observed the Keith caller. "Now, far aboot did ye say this place wis again?"

"Estonia."

"Estonia? Is that near Methlick?"

FANS OF "Francie and Josie" will know that the
late Jack Milroy, who played "Francie" to Rikki
Fulton's "Josie", was one of those rare people in
Scottish variety theatre who had a healthy sense of
his place in the world. Unlike many of his variety
contemporaries, Jack never believed his own publicity
and always had time for people.

When he turned up at His Majesty's Theatre,
Aberdeen, for a gala evening to celebrate the theatre's
refurbishment, a reporter from *The Press and Journal*
inquired if he was still as busy as ever.

"Still just as busy, son," Jack said. "You know
that Rikki's written his autobiography. Well, I've
started writing mine."

"And when will it be out?" said the *P&J* man.

"Don't know. I'm up to page 14 and I've only
covered the family moving four strects from one
house to the other when I was two year aul."

"That's an awful lot of pages to cover one flit-
ting," the *P&J* man joked.

"I know, son," Jack said, "but the traffic wis terrible."

IN THE late 1980s, *The Press and Journal* hired a
freelance journalist from Ireland with the lovely
Gaelic first name Grainne (pronounced Gronya).

Her first outing to a press conference proved too
much of a challenge for North-east security opera-
tives, however. Grainne returned to the office
explaining that she had been late for the start of the
conference because she was delayed by the following
exchange with a security man who had difficulty
spelling.

"Fit's yer first name?"

"Grainne."

"Spell it."

"G-R-A-I-N-N-E."

"Greenie?"

"Not Greenie. Grainne."

"G-R-E? . . ."

"G-R-A-I-N-N-E."

"Groany?"

"Grainne."

"Ach," he said, waving her through. "I'll jist ca ye Darlin."

THE ABERDEEN JOURNALS Inverness office staff tell of a crew from Sky TV arriving in Inverness on one of their periodic visits to check Highland reactions to various news stories. The crew spotted a likely interviewee in Academy Street, so the reporter approached and said: "Excuse me, have you got a few words for Sky TV?"

"I have," snapped the man. "Stick your microphone up your own nose and bugger off back to Portree."

Aches and Pains

Some of the best humour comes when the guard is down. Doctors and nurses are usually the best witnesses on such occasions.

ONE OF Aberdeenshire's most celebrated chemists before World War II was Alexander Sim Weir, who dispensed pills and potions at Kemnay and was known throughout mid-Donside as "Aul Phizz". His contemporaries were Jim Stephen, the postmaster, and Miss Burnett, a very prim and proper old lady.

Miss Burnett was exceptionally fond of her pet Scottie, although she resented the 7/6d that the annual dog licence cost. She appeared at Jim Stephen's post office one afternoon and asked for her licence. When she was told the price, she remarked: "An awful lot for such a small dog."

Unimpressed, Jim returned: "If ye wint onythin chaeper, ging doon tae 'Aul Phizz' for tippence o pooshin."

RETIRED LORRY driver Bill Duncan, of Aberlour, had been warned by his doctor that he would have to moderate his diet and step up the exercise, because a lifetime of sitting behind the wheel had made him a prime candidate for a heart attack.

"Fit exercise wid ye be thinkin o?" he inquired of the doctor.

"Walking, swimming, anything that gets you active," the medical man said. "You're also very weak in your upper arms, so I suggest you take two five-pound tattie bags every morning, one in each hand, and stretch out your arms until they're pointing straight out from your body. Hold them there for five seconds, then let them down slowly. Repeat that five times every morning for a fortnight, then move on to ten-pound tattie bags and do that for another fortnight. Then come back and see me."

When the month was over, Bill returned to the doctor and pronounced himself feeling grand. The doctor examined him and noticed that there didn't appear to have been much change in the blood pressure, the waistline, the upper arms or anything else.

"Have you been lifting the tattie bags like I told you?" he asked.

"Michty aye," Bill said. "In fact, I'm deein that weel I'll maybe pit some tatties in them next wikk."

WE WON'T be identifying which village surgery in the North-east hosted the following conversation (for obvious reasons), but our source explained that it involved a chat between two elderly women who thought that their GP fancied himself as a bit of a matinée idol.

"In fact," said one, "ivry time he taks a wifie's pulse, he taks aff 10 beats tae accoont for her bein sae excited."

NORTH-EAST hospitals are now reporting the discovery of a new Class A drug exclusive to Aberdeen.

Kenfitamine.

Kenfitamine: a new Class A drug
exclusive to Aberdeen

AULD JIMMY had spent most of his life in the North-east as a farm labourer. Living on his own, he avoided most of the comforts of modern living but, eventually, he needed to be taken into residential care, where he maintained some of his old habits.

His major pastime was to clap his bunnet on his head, pull on his beets and go for a walk in the grounds. One day, while he was out for a walk, his neighbour in the adjoining room had a 14-inch black-and-white TV set installed in his room.

Jimmy returned just as the nurse, David Sharp (who sent us the tale and is now living in Ohio), was explaining the controls to the TV's new owner.

"Come and tak a look at this, Jimmy," David said, and, as Jimmy stood wide-eyed, David flipped through the three channels to demonstrate how the set worked. For someone who hadn't had mains water or electricity for most of his life, Jimmy found this almost supernatural.

"Michty," he said. "What a machine. Dis it work aff the gas?"

A BANFFSHIRE farmer turned up at the Aberchirder doctor one day and dropped his dungars to reveal an angry red weal in the shape of a hoofprint on his backside. "I wis kickit," he explained.

In the course of the treatment, the GP asked if the farmer had had many such experiences, and the old boy said he hadn't had any at all in a lifetime's farming.

After a pause, he recounted tales of being flattened by a ram, tossed over fences by bulls and having his leg broken by an angry billy goat.

"Wouldn't you call those accidents?" said the doctor.

"Na," said the farmer. "I think they meant it."

A WRI member from Buchan told us she was once at a talk given by the local GP. He spoke about developments in medicine and then invited questions from the floor.

The first question, prepared in advance in case the ladies were too shy to start themselves, came from the institute president. "Does the doctor think there is any truth in the old saying that an apple a day keeps the doctor away?"

The doctor cleared his throat to answer, but was beaten by a shout from the back of the hall: "Only if yer aim's good."

NOT QUITE a doctoring story, this one, but it's close enough. A vet's nurse from the Banffshire coast (that's close enough) told us that an ability to act was essential for vets who had to deal with children who were deeply upset by the loss of their pets.

One of her employers managed to seem wholly sympathetic while the owners were in the room, but the mood changed as soon as the child or children left.

One day, a hamster that was decidedly past its best was pronounced DOA and the child was dispatched to the arms of her waiting mum.

When the door shut, the vet said: "They'd be as well taking a disposable lighter in for a service."

MEDICAL SECRETARY Isabel Falconer wrote to tell us of her father-in-law, who had no time for doctors and was proud of never having needed medical attention in more than 70 years.

A cough that had persisted for months saw Isabel and her husband drag the thrawn old boy to the GP, who diagnosed something bronchial and prescribed a mixture.

Isabel arranged to deliver the script to the town chemist and collect the mixture herself, despite the patient's insistence that he was perfectly capable of collecting his own medicine. She suspected that he would throw away the prescription when he thought no one was looking. She returned with the medicine and stayed to watch him take the first dose.

By Hogmanay, the cough was no better, so Isabel asked him if he had been taking his mixture.

"I've been deein exactly fit it says on the label," he said, folding his arms.

The label read: Keep Tightly Closed.

LONG AGO, medical services in the North-east were somewhat patchy. For a long time, the only trained doctor between Aberdeen and Huntly was Dr James Milne, of Inverurie.

Although doctors were few and far between, many of the parish ministers and some of the lairds kept stocks of medicines for curing and relieving parishioners. Here and there, too, there were other skeely men and women who were reputed to have a rudimentary knowledge of medicine.

One such woman was the wife of a laird and was

in the habit of collecting wild herbs from round about, to use as medicine among her husband's tenants. When Dr Milne got to hear of it, he demanded to know how she knew that the herbs were not poisonous.

"I ken fine," she snapped, "because I try them on the Laird first."

ONE OF the most celebrated doctors and surgeons the North-east has produced was Alexander Cran, born in Rhynie, educated in London and then beginning practice in Tarland.

His practice was 20 miles across and he earned a reputation as a caring doctor who fought his way through all sorts of hazards and storms, sometimes on horseback or even on foot, to make sure that his patients were looked after.

One wintry night, there was a knocking at his door. A servant opened up and cried: "Fa's there?"

"It's me," said a male voice. "I'm sikkin the doctor tae Babbie, bit dinna hurry him; it's a lang road."

The doctor dressed and set out with the man, asking: "Is there anybody with your wife?"

"Na, doctor," said the man. "I'm nae sikkin ither wifies in aboot. They'll spile wir hoose and eat aa wir jam."

ONE CORRESPONDENT who wishes to remain anonymous recalled taking a newly-wed neighbour to the village doctor in the late 1950s because the girl was too shy to go herself and wanted company in the consulting room.

The doctor asked at one point: "And what about your bowels?"

The lassie seemed mystified and said: "On the shelf abeen the sink."

RETIRED GP Frank Keir asserts, after a lifetime's experience of general practice in the North-east, that there are four grades of illness in the Doric.

1. I'm nae weel.
2. I'm nae affa weel.
3. I'm affa nae weel.
4. I'd be better aff awa.

FRANK ALSO had to deal with a notorious hypochondriac who was worried that she was developing an incurable throat condition. He peered into the depths, but could see nothing worse than an inflammation, so he applied some salve and gave her a prescription for a mixture. She was distinctly dischuffed.

She left the consulting room and walked towards the waiting-room, where her friend was waiting for her. As she left, Frank heard the friend asking her: "Foo did ye get on?"

"Ach," said the patient. "Wisna worth ma while comin. He jist pentit ma throat."

"And fit wis ye expectin?" inquired the chum. "Wallpaper?"

ON ANOTHER occasion, Frank was confronted by a man who nowadays would be called clinically obese. The patient was carrying so much weight in front of him that his back was almost at breaking point. Frank suggested not only a diet, but also a little light exercise, starting small and building up week by week.

The man was horrified. "Exercise?" he said, as if Frank had proposed that the patient sleep in a bed of snakes.

"Nothing drastic," Frank said. "I'm not suggesting you run a full marathon this afternoon. Try something simple at the outset."

"Like fit?"

"Well, why not see how close you can get to touching your toes?"

The patient shook his head. "Na, doctor," he said. "If the good Lord hid meant me tae touch ma taes, he'd hiv put them on ma knees."

AN ELGIN correspondent who once nursed at Dr Gray's Hospital recalled one cantankerous long-stay patient who found fault with absolutely everything. The food was swill, the staff were unfriendly, the ward was cold, the bed was hard.

"One day, during a staff handover," she wrote, "it fell to me to give him a bed-bath. I wasn't looking forward to tholing the torrent of moans.

"Sure enough, as I was dichting one side of him, he was barely drawing breath between complaints. I had almost had enough when he said: 'The trouble wi this place is ye treat aa us patients like dogs.'

"And that was when I heard myself saying: 'Och, that's nonsense, Willie. Now roll over.'"

SANDY NIXON, a doctor in Ayrshire, recalled a North-east exile arriving to live near his practice.

The first time the two met, Sandy had just come out of hospital himself and the new patient was anxious that his new medical man was in fine fettle. "I hear ye've been in the hospital," the North-east man said. "I have that," Sandy said. "Fit wis adee, like?" "A perforated bowel." "A perforated bowel? Michty, far I come fae, we ca that a colander."

ONE ANONYMOUS correspondent wrote with a tale of taking her youngest daughter to the doctor, who sounded the little girl's chest with a stethoscope.

When they returned home, the girl rushed to her father and cried: "Dad! Dad! The doctor pits his galluses in his lugs!"

RETIRED NURSE Pam Oliphant had a hand in nurse training in Aberdeen and the North-east for more than 40 years and kept notes of some of the howlers in student reports, including:

Patient's father died in his nineties of ladies' troubles in his prostate.

On the second day, her knee appeared much improved. By the third day it had disappeared completely.

Patient is numb from her toes down.

Patient complains of extreme pain when his head is rotated through 360°.

Patient is a healthy-appearing but decrepit male, 69, who is mentally alert but forgetful.

Patient complains of occasional, constant, infrequent headaches.

Examination of genitalia was completely negative, except for soreness in the right foot.

By the time patient was admitted, his rapid heart had stopped and he was feeling better.

An X-ray was conducted of patient's head, but nothing was found.

Patient's skin was moist and dry.

Patient has no past history of suicides.

Examination of patient's genitalia revealed that he was circus-sized.

Patient has no shakes or obvious temperature chills, but her husband says she was really hot in bed last night.

Law and Order

The due process of law in all its forms has a healthy sense of humour. You just need to ask any bobby, lawyer or prison officer, which is exactly what we did.

THIS TALE came to us via HM Prison, Craiginches, Aberdeen – "Craigie" to its regular residents – so we have no doubt as to its accuracy.

In the late 1980s, a prison van was bringing another batch of miscreants from the cells at Aberdeen High Court; all the culprits were about to start their various sentences.

The occupants of the back of the van were the usual motley collection, but one stuck out as being different: a greying, middle-aged man in an impeccable suit, and impressively coiffed and manicured. The regulars were studying him intently, but he didn't catch their looks and instead stared blankly as if he were the only one in the vehicle.

"Fit's the boy in for?" inquired an old lag of one of the prison officers.

"He looks like a paedophile tae me," said another.

"Be quiet," said the officer.

Then the chant got up: "Pae-do! Pae-do! Pae-do!"

"Be quaet!" barked the senior officer. "It's neen o yer damned business, bit he murdered his wife."

An instant hush fell over the van as the inmates absorbed this new information. The quiet was broken only by one voice muttering: "Dis he dee homers?"

ONE OF the most celebrated felons Scotland has seen was Harry McGlashan, who, in the North-east vernacular, was an affa takkin mannie, in both senses of the word: he pinched anything he could lay his hands on, but he was charm personified whenever he was caught – which was often.

One sheriff peered at Harry in the dock for the umpteenth time and sighed: "McGlashan," he said. "Do you have any intention of ever finding a job?"

Harry shuffled uneasily.

"You could train for a trade," the sheriff said. "Thousands of people do."

"Nae me, sir," McGlashan said.

"Why ever not? Have you tried?"

"No, sir. I'm nae affa bright."

A FARM worker had decided to take his former employer to an industrial tribunal, claiming unfair dismissal, according to Ackie Manson, of Oldmeldrum.

"Are you saying," inquired the tribunal chairman, "That you were not fairly dismissed?"

"Michty, aye," said the farm worker. "That's fit wye I'm here. Fairly, I wis dismissed."

NOW two tales from a former bobby Down South who has retired back to Deeside and who requests anonymity. You'll understand why.

On his retirement from the force, never having risen from the rank of constable, our man was surprised to hear that the Chief Constable wanted to make the farewell presentation personally at the force HQ with all his colleagues.

"Now, Jack," said the top man, "I sent your Division Superintendent out to buy a suitable present for you. He said it would be difficult as you have done 35 years' service and it would need a robot to replace you.

"'Aha,' I thought. 'A robot as a retirement gift.' But the Superintendent couldn't find a robot that did bugger all."

THEN THERE was the Deeside bobby (not our Jack) who had also spent a large part of his career Down South, and who had become over-fond of a drammie or three during his time in exile. The Chief Constable got to hear of his alcohol problem and called him in for a chat.

The Chief suggested that the bobby take some extended leave and head back to his hame airt for a cure.

"I'm nae sure that'll stop me wi the drink, sir," said the disconsolate bobby.

"Probably not," said the Chief, "But at least up there you won't stand out in a crowd."

ONE OF the legends of the Elgin law community is the tale from Elgin Sheriff Court in the 1920s when a tinkie wife was charged with public drunkenness. The court convened; the accused stood in the dock, and the charge was read out in the form of the day: "The procurator fiscal complains that . . ."

At that, the tinkie wife snapped: "Ach, thon bugger's aye complainin."

PETERHEAD SHERIFF COURT has always hosted some of the North-east's more exotic trials, including one recalled by a former Aberdeen Journals reporter in the town.

It was more or less a simple assault case, but both parties wanted their day in court, so a ten-minute shoo-through became a full-blown Perry Mason job.

It boiled down to the fact that two men at a factory in the town had had a discussion about how best to approach a particular job. The discussion became an argument. The argument became a push-and-shove match. The push and shove became a fight.

In court, Wullie's solicitor asked for his client's version of events. "Weel, yer honour," Wullie said. "I canna myn exactly, bit Frunkie and me hid an argument. Frunkie says I wisna deein ma job richt. I says I wis. Then he hut me. So I hut him. Then Frunkie says tae me: 'If you !@£$%^&! touch me again, I'll !@£$%^&! kill ye'."

"I see," said the solicitor. "And when your colleague said to you: 'If you !@£$%^&! touch me again, I'll !@£$%^&! kill ye', what did you take him to mean?"

ONE OF our overseas correspondents, Jimmie Walker, who resides in Oliver, British Columbia, told of a lawyer named Malcolm McDougall back home in Scotland. Mr McDougall was sitting in his office working his way through a pile of papers, when there was a sharp rap at the door and a burly woman entered, dragging her teenage daughter behind her.

They sat down, still unbidden, and the mother

explained that her daughter had just been found to be pregnant and that they wanted to sue the man responsible.

Mr McDougall pushed his pile of work to one side and took a fresh sheet of paper. Pen poised, he said: "All right, let's see. What's the man's name?"

The girl leaned across. "I'm affa sorry," she said. "I didna ken him personally."

WE'RE OBLIGED to Ally Spence for telling us of the country bobby who encountered a lad who had been knocking spots off the bottle all night and was now hytering and stytering home along the pavement. Two steps forward, one step back. Two steps left, one step right.

"Aye, Jim," the bobby said. "That's you makkin yer wye hame."

"Weel," Jim slurred. "Fyles."

WHEN LENA McPHERSON'S late husband was a young bobby in Moray, he would often do school talks. At one such event, at Burghead, he had to mention a number of acts of vandalism in the area, and suggested that if any of the children saw anything of that sort happening again, they should tell a grown-up or contact the police themselves.

The talk had gone reasonably well, Mr McPherson thought, and as he was leaving after his fly cup with the staff, he spotted a small girl waiting anxiously at the school gate. "Could I spik tae ye?" she said as he approached.

He squatted down beside her.

"My mam says a bobby will aye help me if I'm in trouble," she said.

Mr McPherson nodded. "Nivver be scared tae spik tae a bobby," he said.

"Well," she said. "wid ye tie ma laces?"

AT THE height of atomic-bomb hysteria, there was great discussion throughout Scotland about civil-defence measures and what might have to be done if the Big One dropped.

This worry manifested itself in many ways, but the one that former bobby Ian Sandison remembers best arose when he was giving a talk on crime prevention to a WRI on the south side of Aberdeen and asked for questions. One woman asked if Ian had advice on what to do in the event of nuclear attack.

"It was a bit of a challenge for a young bobby," Ian said, "and a bit of a cheek for me to answer, since I knew nothing about it apart from what I'd read. However, I recalled an advice leaflet that I'd seen at HQ, so I explained what to do if you were caught in a building."

"That's fine if ye're inside," one woman said, "bit fit if ye're ootside; say, in yer gairden?"

"Well," Ian said, "The official advice is to find a hollow, lie down and pull leaves over as much of yourself as possible."

"Ach, fit eese wid that be?" snapped the woman.

"Well, Ina," said her friend, "at least ye'd leave a tidy gairden."

KENNY KEIR was a young traffic constable in the

days of the old Aberdeen City Police and was directing traffic when the lights had failed at the junction of Bridge Street and Union Street.

He was calmly attending to the flow on Union Street when he heard a screech of tyres behind him and an almighty bang. A Vauxhall Victor being driven by a young blonde had been in collision with a fruit van driven by an older man in a brown shopcoat. Both drivers leapt out and started a shouting match.

Kenny did his best to keep the traffic moving, while shouting at the pair to calm down and behave themselves, although he had a hard time not laughing when he heard the man tell the woman: "You should stick tae drivin a pram."

"Aye," she said. "And you should be in it."

"Stick tae drivin a pram"

Please, Miss

Schools, like shoppies and pubs, are natural sources of humour, and teachers have a ringside seat. Here are the best examples of the often accidental wit that arises in the classroom and staffroom.

A RESIDENT of the Woodend area of Aberdeen, who asks to remain anonymous, was proud that both her sons got good degrees, but was especially proud when Donald managed his doctorate and was summoned to the US to give a lecture in his field of expertise.

Alas, some of the family's older friends didn't quite grasp how time had passed and how wee Donald had grown up. When one such elderly lady asked where Donald was, his mum replied: "He's away in Florida delivering a paper."

"Really?" said the woman. "An affa lang wye tae deliver a paper. Hiv they nae paper loons o their ain?"

A PRIMARY-SCHOOL teacher from Perth, who asks to be known only as Pat, says she seated her charges round about her one December morning to read them the nativity story.

She was about five minutes into proceedings when she heard a small voice mutter: "Ach, this is the same story we got last year."

OLDER TEACHERS among you will remember that school policy in most Scottish education authorities

"He's away in Florida delivering a paper."

after the war was that pupils had to empty their pockets onto the teacher's desk before break time and collect their belongings on their return.

One day, a threepenny bit had "gone missing" from one school in, shall we say, a deprived area of Aberdeen.

Teacher waited until the class returned, then said: "Now, children, we've had a bad fairy in the room during playtime, I think. She has made a threepenny piece disappear from my desk.

"Why don't we all lay our heads down on our desks, put our hands over our heads, keep our eyes tightly shut and wish very hard for the bad fairy to come back with the threepence. Let's all do that, shall we? And let's promise not to peek in case she decides not to come."

Teacher led by example and the class followed. Within a few seconds, she felt a soft poke–poke at her shoulder, heard a coin being slid across her desk, and heard a small voice whispering: "She must hiv put it in my pooch, the bitch."

RETIRED EDUCATION lecturer Bob Cooper taught in Kincardine and Angus in the 1960s and recalled trying one day to teach a class of 13 boys who were not academically gifted.

Like many teachers before him, Bob resorted to apple analogies. "David, if your mother and father were to share one apple, into how many bits would your mum cut it?"

"Twa."

"That's right. And each would be called? . . ."

"A half."

"Good. Alan, if you, your mother, your father and your sister were to share an apple, how many bits would your mum need to cut?"

"Fower."

"And each would be called? . . ."

"A quaaarter."

The lesson was going well until one lad, Raymond, interrupted. "Bit, sir, there's eicht o's in oor faimly."

Bob was secretly delighted, because the question of eighths had arisen unprompted. "All right," he said to his class; "here's Raymond with eight in his family. What does his mum have to do?"

One boy shot up his hand. "Get twa aipples."

LATER in Bob's career, in Angus, he found himself with a class of what, today, would be termed special-needs pupils. One of them, Brian, with an IQ of about 70, was having a bad day. He couldn't draw a square, despite help. He couldn't give the months of the year, and had great difficulty with the days of the week.

Before giving up completely, Bob thought he would try to touch on a subject which might evoke some meaningful response.

"Tell me, Brian," he said. "Who won the Derby yesterday?"

"Tae tell ye the truth, Mr Cooper," Brian said. "I'm nae really interestit in fitba."

ONE OF the sweetest people the North-east has produced was Lilianne Grant Rich, teacher, devoted daughter of the area and latterly a fine writer and poet.

Lilianne had a healthy sense of fun and often recalled her teaching days in the farther-flung rural airts. At one such two-teacher school, Lilianne often had to do double duty and was one day heading the cookery class. She found herself preparing a vegetable medley, mostly using old foodstuffs from her own larder because the school budget wouldn't run to buying fresh.

She confessed later that the results weren't quite what she had hoped, but she presented the finished dish to the class with a theatrical flourish and asked: "Now, boys and girls, does anyone know what we call this?"

From half-way up the classroom she heard a low voice: "Well, in oor hoose we'd ca it a bliddy kirn, bit you please yersel."

ONCE, WHEN a representative of His Majesty's Inspectorate was paying a professional call, Lilianne, like all teachers, was on edge in case the class misbehaved. Things appeared to be going well at the introduction stage. All the pupils duly stood and chimed: "Good morning, sir", as had been prescribed.

She experienced a flash of panic when, as the inspector was looking round for a spare chair at the edge of the class, young Ian shot up from his own seat, ran to the other side of the room and retrieved a stool that was designed more for a pupil than a burly chap in his forties.

Nevertheless, the inspector thanked him kindly. "Nae bother," said Ian, heading back to his seat. "I

"Boys and girls, does anyone know
what we call this?"

wis feart ye'd pick that big cheir in the corner and there's a nail in it that wid ca the erse fae yer brikks."

A TEACHER from Mintlaw got in touch to say that several years ago when she was setting a wee geography test for her pupils, one of her questions was: "How are clouds formed?"

One returned paper included the answer: "I am not sure how clouds are formed, but as long as the clouds know, that is the important thing."

PRIMARY TEACHER Sonia Murren was teaching a playful assortment of five-year-olds and had drawn the discussion round to the alphabet. The first child was required to give the first letter of the alphabet, the second the second, and so on.

All went well until he came to the 16th child, who confessed eventually that he was stumped.

"Come on," Miss Murren said. "What comes after O?"

After a moment, a voice from the back offered: "Yeah."

ABERDEEN PRIMARY-SCHOOL teacher Mary Rennie asked her charges to write about their saddest day. One pupil, Colin, delivered an essay about visiting a graveyard for the first time, which included the line: "It was very sad to see so many people lying in peas."

Mary also recalled the last day of term before the Christmas holidays when she asked her class what song they would like to sing. There was silence for a moment, then one wee girl's hand shot up. "Please, miss, could we sing Miniza's Song?"

"Miniza's Song? Miniza who?"

"Don't know, miss."

"Well, how does it go?"

The little lass cleared her throat and began: "Miniza seen the glory of the coming of the Lord . . ."

IT'S ENCOURAGING to find in archives 200 years old that there is evidence of Doric wit. According to education records, a farmer living in the Glens o Foudland at the start of the nineteenth century told the local dominie that his daughter would not be allowed to learn to read or write as "she'll mak ill eese o't and jist start writin tae lads".

ONE OLDMELDRUM teacher in the early 1960s had asked her mainly rural pupils to write a short essay about a happy event that had occurred at home in the previous week. One such essay explained: "My father has bought a new raping machine. It does the work of five men."

ANOTHER OLDMELDRUM teacher tells of inviting a tourist-information officer to talk to a class of 13-year-olds about why tourism is so vital to the economy of Scotland, and why tourists should be treated royally.

When the call went out for questions, one perceptive young lad asked if the tourist-information officer approved of caravanners.

"We like anyone who comes here," the man said.

"Everyone's welcome. Why do you ask about cara-vanners?"

At that point, it became clear that the young lad's family had a vested interest in the tourism business. "Because," the boy said, "ma dad says caravanners is parasites. He says they arrive wi a £10 note, a pair o socks and a shirt and they nivver change ony o them."

THE SAME teacher recalled a Monday-morning class when she was a primary-school teacher and picked up the buzz in the classroom that one of her pupils had suffered a tragedy over the weekend.

She asked the boy to stay behind at playtime, and broached the subject gently. Yes, he said, it was true that there had been a death in the household. The family dog had passed away in its sleep on the Saturday night, so the rest of the weekend had been extremely sad for all concerned.

The teacher empathised, for she had lost two dogs in similar circumstances, but advised from experi-ence that the best cure was to go right out and get another dog.

"We're deein that this wikk," the boy said.

"Well, that's good," the teacher said. "You'll never forget the old one, but you have the new one to look forward to."

"Aye," the boy said, making to go. Then he turned. "Ma faither says if it wis atween a new dog and a new wife, he wid tak the dog ivry time, for a dog's aye pleased tae see ye."

JIM EWEN was a principal teacher of physics at a celebrated North-east academy and still revels in the antics of a particularly difficult janitor, who ruled the school as if it was his own. Neither was the jannie afraid to stand up to authority.

Jim witnessed the rector approaching the jannie one day and asking him to move some flower tubs for the sake of safety. The janitor refused, adding: "Look, I can only please ae body a day. The day isna your day."

He paused for dramatic effect and added: "And the morn's nae lookin good eether."

THE LATE grandmother of Aberdeen PR executive Neil Robertson was an English teacher at Peterhead Academy, who used to enjoy telling of her first encounter with a particular class that was, shall we say, less academically inclined.

As usual in such circumstances, she asked the class to introduce themselves, so off they set, in desk order. Eventually, the self-introductions came to one big bruiser.

"Robert Red, miss," he said.

"Red?" she said. "Robert Red? That's a strange name."

"Weel, miss," he said, "it's really Robert Reid, bit ma mither says I've tae start spikkin better."

WHEN FAMED HM Inspector Dr Kerr was examining a country school near Huntly early last century, he decided to test the knowledge of one class about the usefulness of animals.

"What," he asked one boy, "does the ox produce?"

"Beef."

"And what does the sheep produce?"

"Mutton.

"Yes, but what else does the sheep produce?"

The boy hesitated, looking nervous, so Dr Kerr took hold of the sleeve of the boy's jacket and said: "Well, what is this made of?"

The boy seemed unwilling to give an answer, but Dr Kerr insisted, and at last the boy admitted tearfully that his jacket was made "oot o ma faither's aul brikks".

A SICK NOTE from an Elgin direction read: "Please excuse Gary for not being at the school on Monday. I've been upside down with the painters all weekend."

Good for the Soul

A lively sense of humour is a valuable asset to men and women of the cloth, and many of their stories were among the most colourful we were offered.

RETIRED trawlerman George Buchan recalled sitting in a Fraserburgh hostelry one evening, a few years back, trying to console a neighbour whose daughter's marriage had just broken up, whose dog had been run over the previous week and whose mother-in-law was about to visit for the entire summer.

"Ye're nae haein muckle luck aenoo, min," George soothed.

"No," said the companion, reaching for another swig of his pint. "Frankly, George, I think I hid a curse put on me ae day 30 year ago."

George wasn't sure if a punchline was coming or if his neighbour truly believed in the black arts, so he pressed further. "Really?"

"Aye," said the neighbour. "April 14 1956."

"Fit kinna curse, like?" George asked.

"Well, as far as I can mind, the minister said: 'I now pronounce you man and wife.'"

THE REVEREND James Simpson used to tell of consoling a small boy whose grandfather had died, and explaining that the old man was now safe in the arms of God and Jesus.

The same small boy was dispatched to see Mr Simpson a few months later and explained through sobs that his goldfish had died.

"I now pronounce you man and wife"

"Well, well," the minister said. "Don't you worry about that. Your goldfish is safe in the arms of Jesus."

Far from consoling the boy, this news sent him into uncontrollable howls, alarming Mr Simpson.

"Mercy me," said the minister, "What's ado?"

"Ma goldfish," sobbed the boy. "Jesus'll feed him tae the five thoosan."

MR SIMPSON also recalled the household where the husband had died and had been laid out in the front room for neighbours to come and pay their respects. He had been a notoriously bad husband and a grouchy individual with virtually everyone in the area all his life. As is the North-east way, however, all of that was conveniently forgotten in death.

Indeed, neighbours poured out eulogy after eulogy as they stood in the kitchen, drinking tea and nibbling biscuits.

The widow sat patiently at the table; then, when she could stand it no longer, she got up and made for the lobby door. "Excuse me," she said, "I'm awa ben the hoose. I jist wint tae see if it really is John that's deid."

A PORTGORDON stalwart wanted to tell us of a celebrated tale from Fochabers Sunday School, where the teacher had been explaining to her charges that "Jesus was a man of peace."

She waited for a few seconds to let the information have full effect, then asked: "Now, does anyone know what that means?"

A hand shot up. "Please, miss. It means he likit loaf."

THE REVEREND Jimmy Smith, whose charge took in vast swathes of Donside, told of an older and much sterner colleague of the cloth who spotted a man rolling and singing in the gutter at Kemnay one New Year before the war.

"Good gracious, man," said the minister. "Is that bottle the only consolation you have left in the world?"

"No," said the drunk. "I've anither een in ma pooch."

THE LATE John Mearns used to tell of a young couple visiting his nearby manse to discuss their marriage plans and the wedding arrangements. As they left, the minister's parting advice on the doorstep was: "Oh, and dinna forget the banns."

"We're nae needin a bann," said the groom-to-be. "A fiddle and melodeon'll dee's fine."

THE SENSE of humour of the clergy sometimes manifests itself in delightful ways. For several weeks in 1991, a church in Holburn Street, Aberdeen, had the following billboard in its grounds:

WHEN THE DAY OF RECKONING COMES
WILL YOU BE SMOKING
OR NON-SMOKING?

THE LATE Reverend James Davidson, who was possessed of a fine and twinkling sense of humour, recalled visiting Market Place School, Inverurie, one day in the 1960s and speaking to a class of seven-year-olds.

"Now, who says grace at home?" he asked, but there was complete puzzlement on the children's faces.

"Do you say prayers before you eat?" Mr Davidson explained.

"No," came a small voice from the back. "My mummy's a good cook."

WE HAD better not reveal the location for the next tale, nor the name of his church, but when he was a young minister doing relief pulpit duty, he had to begin one of his preaching to one Donside congregation by apologising for the shortness of his sermon. He explained that one of his puppies had eaten a couple of the pages of his prepared text that morning.

At the end of the service, one of the locals approached him and inquired: "Ye widna hae a spare pup for wir usual minister, wid ye?"

WE'RE OBLIGED to North-east exile Mrs Leslie Finnie, now of Neilston, near Glasgow, who recalled a young minister arriving in her old Buchan country parish between the wars and going for a walk round his new flock. He came upon a very old woman hyowin neeps in a park.

After introducing himself, he professed admiration for her being able to do such hard work at her age, and asked: "Have you no family to help you?"

"Aye" she replied, "I've three braw loons, though

they're aa set up in places o their ain and they canna aye be at my biddin."

"I see," said the minister. "Have you been a widow for very long?"

She stopped her work and looked up. "Bless ye, Meenister," she said. "I wis nivver mairriet."

"But I thought you said you had three sons."

"Aye," she said. "I wis nivver mairriet, bit I wis nivver negleckit."

IN THE 1913 edition of *Bygone Days in Aberdeenshire*, the author recalled a church beadle who dug a grave to accommodate the remains of a niggardly farmer's wife.

When the interment was complete, the farmer said that he was obliged to the beadle for the trouble that he had taken.

"Oh," said the beadle, "there's nae sense in bein obliged tae me. It's jist fower and saxpence."

"Fower and saxpence!" the farmer spluttered. "I thocht you beadles did this for nithing."

"Faith, nivver," said the beadle. "I jist gets fower and saxpence."

"I'll gie ye half a croon," the farmer said.

"No," the beadle said firmly. "It's fower and saxpence."

"Please yersel," the farmer said. "If ye dinna tak half a croon, ye get nithing ata."

"Fine," said the beadle as he rammed his spade into the new ground. "Up she comes."

He got his fower and saxpence.

ANOTHER BEADLE from the turn of the nineteenth into the twentieth century was showing a woman round the church one day. When the visit drew to a close, the woman offered her guide profound thanks and headed for the gate.

"Weel, ma lady," the beadle said after her, "fin ye ging hame, if ye find oot that ye've lost yer purse, I hope ye myn that ye didna hae it oot here."

BEFORE THE war, the Reverend John Davidson got wind of a rumour that one of his beadles at King Edward had overcharged for the burial of a well-known farmer, so he challenged the beadle for the truth.

"Weel, sir," the beadle said, "that fairmer eence took a nip o me wi the price o a calf, an I nivver got a chunce tae get ma ain back."

THE same minister was preparing for Sunday sermon and became aware that the bell appeared to be ringing for a lot longer than usual.

He stepped out of the vestry to find the beadle yarking on the rope, oblivious to all around him. He tapped the beadle on the shoulder and said: "The bell's ringing quite a while this morning, beadle."

"Aye, sir," the beadle said, with a flick of his thumb towards the body of the kirk. "Ye hinna muckle fowk in the day, and I'm jist makkin sure the rest's nae aa at hame sleepin."

SHORTLY BEFORE the war, a kirk at Foggieloan found itself with a visitor in the pews at Sunday

Sermon. "A queer-like English gadgie," wrote our correspondent, "but whenever the minister stopped to draw breath, the visitor would clap his hands and shout: 'Praise the Lord! Hallelujah!'

"This drawing attention to himself was some much for the good folk o Foggie, so there was a great deal of muttering and disapproving scowls until three elders took it upon themselves to go back to the visitor and whisper: 'Jist behave yersel. We dinna praise the Lord here.'"

Mony a Gweed Tune

The older generation is one of the richest humour sources of all, mostly because they have far more years to call on. Once again, this was the chapter for which the keep-in / leave-out decision was most difficult.

THE BLOOD TRANSFUSION SERVICE runs periodic trips round the North-east countryside, setting up mobile centres in school car parks and community halls to collect pints of the best from country arms.

At one such stop, Sheila, one of the nurses, explained to an older female donor that the blood was vital to the country and that the woman was performing a great service.

"I hope so," said the woman. "Tell me, fit happens tae the bleed efter it leaves here?"

"Well," Sheila said. "It goes for testing first."

"Testing?"

"Well, you know, Aids and viruses and things."

The woman was suddenly horrified. "ye're testin my bleed for Aids?"

"It's just routine."

"Well," humphed the woman, "ye're wastin yer time testin my bleed for Aids. I dinna ging oot at nicht."

RETIRED BUS-DRIVER Alan Ogg remembers the long-standing love–hate relationship involving his father and one of his father's closest pals, who lived across the road in Kittybrewster, Aberdeen.

"Ye're wastin yer time testin my bleed for Aids."

"Bill and my dad had been through school together, through the war together, raised their families together and done everything together," Alan wrote. "They were also hellish stubborn and were prone to falling out and not speaking for weeks, even though both families could see they thought the world of each other and were lifelong devoted pals.

"When Bill, the pal, died in early 2000, my dad was inconsolable. He wouldn't speak to anyone. He was almost angry at Bill for dying on him.

"When we went to see him the day before the funeral, he announced that he wouldn't be going to Bill's funeral. We were astonished and asked him why not.

"'Well,' he said. 'He winna come tae mine.'"

HELEN HENDRY, of Alford, remembers that whenever her stepfather was asked by the bairns what he had been doing, he would reply: "Riddlin rikk and rowin it awa in barras."

SSPCA OFFICERS from various parts of northern Scotland have an important job to do, but they find some calls from older customers especially bewildering.

Among strange callouts in recent years was one from a woman who had spotted a dead horse in a pond. It turned out to be a floating plank. One panicky soul reported a magpie trailing its wing on the hard shoulder of the A90 between Aberdeen and Stonehaven. That was a discarded trainer. Birds trapped in chimneys are usually smoke-alarm batteries running down, says our contact.

One Banffshire pensioner phoned the fire brigade in quite a state because she had spotted a snake sleeping behind her TV and was worried it was going to pounce and bite her if she tried to leave the room. Firemen discovered that the woman's son had strapped together various cables behind the TV into a few loops and coils to make the place look tidier.

Our favourite, however, was the woman who called the police, screaming and crying that she had trapped a wildcat in her bedroom and would someone come quickly because the animal was so angry that it was bound to wreck her furniture and shred her bedding.

The wildcat turned out to be a pair of the old lady's bloomers. It all ended happily, but if her bloomers looked like an angry wildcat it does make you wonder what the woman looked like.

ONE CORRESPONDENT overheard an elderly couple in a Huntly tearoom involved in a heated conversation about religion and asylum-seekers. It will come as no surprise to observers of North-east values that both of them wanted the whole lot repatriated by the boatload, pronto.

As a Parthian shot, the woman added: "Michty, I can mind fin Muslim wis fit wir mither biled clootie dumplin in."

FROM STRATHBOGIE comes the tale of the old crofter dying suddenly and the people of the parish visiting the widow to pay their respects. When one of his old chums turned up, the widow asked if he would like to visit the deceased, who was lying in state in the front room.

"Fairly that."

He was guided through and looked at his old pal for a few moments then observed: "Man, he looks weel enough. There's even a bit smile on his face."

"Ye're richt," the widow said. "Jock wis aye a bittie saft. He disna ken fit's happened til him yet."

ACCOUNTANT IAN JOHNSTON, brought up at Turriff and now living in Aberdeen, recalled visiting his (now-deceased) mother-in-law at Echt when two neighbours arrived with a present for the old lady from their recent holiday in Bangkok.

Had they enjoyed the holiday, the old lady inquired.

"Well, bits o't," said the man. "Though, if we're honest, we were a bittie put aff wi aa the prostitutes and drug dealers and sex shops and ory stuff like that."

The conversation went on for a few minutes more and the couple left. Ian said his mother-in-law turned quiet and looked distressed.

"Fit's adee?" Ian said.

"Ach, I'm nae cut oot for times like this," she said. "I'm ower aul. Fancy haein tae thole that kinna fool dirt on yer holidays."

"Well," Ian said, "that's fit ye've tae expect noo-adays in Thailand."

"Thailand?" said the old lady, brightening. "I thocht they said Tarland."

AN AVID novel-reader near Forres liked long romantic sagas, but discovered as the years wore on that the novels became more and more graphic in their bedroom scenes and left little to the imagination.

Her niece, who told us this story, said that one week when the old lady was otherwise busy, she asked her husband to pick up a selection of new books from the town library. She said he could choose whatever he thought she would like.

Alas, her husband had no idea what she would like, so he sought the advice of the librarian, adding: "Make it something relaxing because she's desperate for a break from non-stop sex."

SEVERAL ELDERLY women were attending a function at Longmorn, near Elgin, and the conversation turned inevitably to one of their contemporaries who had long since left the area.

They began trying to sort out, among half-remembered truths and colourful rumours, the fortunes of the exile since her departure.

"Weel," said one, "I ken she mairried a Jim Aitken."

"Fit?" said another, shocked. "A black mannie?"

BACK IN the 1960s, Grampian TV presenters would spend many a weekend opening this fête and that country fayre. George Innes, of Ellon, reports that after one such event his late mother-in-law, Elsie, returned from an event in the town to announce proudly that she had managed to obtain June Imray's autograph.

"Really?" said George's dad. "Fit dis it say?"

"Well," said his mum. "It says: 'June Imray'."

COOKERY DEMONSTRATOR Mamie Mitchell was looking after her two grandchildren, Beth (4) and Stuart (2). After the usual bedtime story, Mamie discovered that her two charges were still wide awake. What to do?

Mamie said she would sing them some of her favourite Christmas carols until they fell asleep. She started off with *Away in a Manger*, followed that with *Once in Royal David's City*, and was just starting *Silent Night*, when Beth advised:

"You can stop singing now. We're both sleeping."

AN ELGIN reader's elderly aunt was a feisty old bird with a strongly developed sense of social decorum and morality. She visited her nephew some years ago and, late one evening, appeared in the kitchen and asked what "conjugals" were.

Not sure if she could take the truth, he asked why she wanted to know.

"Because there's a play on the TV and I've just heard one man say that he was away home for his conjugals."

"Ah," he said, thinking quickly. "That's a milky drink you have before bedtime."

She appeared quite happy with this explanation, and trotted off.

Two decades later, after her funeral, he was at the biled-ham after the interment and chatting with his late aunt's friends when he learned that, latterly, when she had evening visitors, she had got into the habit of looking pointedly at the mantelpiece clock and telling her guests they would have to go soon as it was nearly time for her conjugals.

TWO WOMEN were overheard travelling on the bus from Banchory to Aberdeen in March 1998. Our source, who was seated in the row behind, says the pair's conversation was a pretty vicious character assassination of someone else, which concluded:

"And she's nae bonnie. Well, nae her face."

Mixter Maxter

On the basis that every good filing system needs a "Miscellaneous" folder, here are all the odds and ends that didn't fit in naturally anywhere else.

ONE OF the tales that has passed into Donside legend comes from the 1950s and the days when a village football team, the Alford Favourites, managed to find themselves a sponsor in the form of one of the community notables. We won't be naming him in order to preserve the peace.

So grateful were the Favourites for the man's generosity that they invited him to make a wee speech from the centre spot and to kick off the first match of the season.

Against a howling gale, the assembled crowds and teams heard the sponsor conclude his address: "It has been a great privilege to support my local team in this way, and I am honoured that you thought of letting me start the game for you. If I'm spared, I hope you'll let me come back in future seasons so I can kick your balls off again."

BILL SANGSTER, former purveyor of cold meats to the gentry, often used to take his dogs for a walk round the Victoria or Westburn parks in the city.

"I never bought a pedigree dog in my life," Bill wrote. "I always went to the dog home for a rescue animal. They always had more character, I thought."

Bill didn't realise how much character until his new signing, Herman, a small terrier of indeterminate breed, was running back and forth one blazing June lunchtime. Another dog-owner stopped to speak to Bill.

"New dog, Bill?" said the other man.

"Aye," Bill said.

"Fit kinna breed wid that be?"

"Well," Bill said. "We're thinkin his father wis a cairn."

"Maybe," said the other man, "and it looks like his mither wisna carin."

OUT ON the oil rigs now, and a Peterhead reader tells of sitting in a recreation room on one platform with three dozen of his mates, all watching a live UEFA Cup match. The half-time adverts started, including one for a red-top tabloid promoting a new feature series.

"This week in *The Sun*," said the voice-over. "Improve your love life on holiday."

An Aberdeen voice called from the back of the room: "Leave the wife at hame."

BACK in the days when crossing the Forth Road Bridge on a motorcycle cost nothing, dedicated sixtysomething biker David Strathcarron was heading north from London on a wee tour to blow the cobwebs out of his system.

He was delighted when he was waved through the tollbooth free of charge at South Queensferry, and headed off across the rolling farmlands of Fife, thoroughly enjoying himself.

"It all came to an end as I approached Dundee,"

"Fit kinna breed wid that be?"

David said. "I stopped at the tollbooth, where the rather surly occupant demanded 20p, I think it was."

"I told him: 'But I was able to cross the Forth Bridge for nothing.'

"'Aye,' said the tollman. 'The farrer north ye come, the mair miserable we are.'"

THE TOUCHING naivete of new young dads is always worth a mention, and Lorna Cormack, of Fraserburgh, wrote to tell us of leaving the Mattie with their first-born. When the Mattie sister asked if there were any last questions, Lorna's husband, Brian, said: "Aye, is there a set time that we should wakken him up in the morning?"

BILL FARQUHAR, of Elgin, was out fishing with his father one Sunday afternoon in the 1950s when an old acquaintance strolled up on the bank and stopped.

"Foo mony hiv ye catched, Sandy?" the friend inquired mischievously, eyeing the empty bag at the two Farquhars' feet.

"Well," said Bill's dad, "if we catch this ane, then we catch anither twa, we'll hae three."

ABERLOUR TAXI-DRIVER Willie Roy was summoned to the Craigellachie Hotel one afternoon. Two Japanese tourists needed to travel the few miles to Dufftown to do some shopping and indulge their passion for all things Scottish. They told Willie they wanted to buy "some really good whisky and some butteries".

Willie thought The Whisky Shop would be the place for a wide selection of drams, but warned that teatime was maybe a bit late to be finding butteries at Dufftown.

He dropped his two charges at The Whisky Shop and decided to do the friendly thing and go and see if he could find some butteries for them. There was none at the baker. None at the newsagent. None at one grocery.

With hope evaporating rapidly, Willie tried another grocer and found possibly the day's last bag of butteries in the whole of Upper Banffshire. He was just on the point of paying when his two guests bowled up.

"I found you some butteries," he said. "The last bag." He held it out to them proudly.

They looked at each other, mystified. "What's that?" asked one, pointing at the North-east's most palatable delicacy.

"That's your butteries," Willie said.

"No," said the pair. "We want butteries. Butteries! For camera!"

JEAN ABERNETHY, of Ellon, was in a restaurant in Aberdeen in the late 1970s, and the service was extremely slow. Indeed, almost every customer in the place was sighing and looking at watches.

The mood lightened considerably, however, when one elderly country chiel stopped a waitress and said: "Excuse me, dearie. Did the lassie that took ma order leave ony next o kin?"

MOTOR BUFFS among you will know of the delights of satellite navigation, the somewhat expensive system fitted to many modern cars which takes triangulation readings from six satellites orbiting the globe and can pinpoint a car's position to within 10 yards and thus guide drivers who are unfamiliar with any given area.

Alas, all this twenty-first-century technology has yet to impress Doric Man.

Car-salesman Bill Pirie was on a test drive with an elderly country chiel and prospective customer. He wheeled off the road, intending to keep the "satnav" as the *coup de théâtre* – the gimmick that would clinch the deal.

The farmer peered at the screen and the display of altitude and of global-positioning in degrees, minutes and seconds. "You'll always know where you are, wherever you are," Bill said proudly.

"Bit I ken far I am," the country chiel said. "I'm in the Tesco car park."

BACK in the dying days of the Buchan Line, the stationmaster at Strichen was worried by a drunk, teetering at the edge of the platform, waiting for the last Saturday-night service to the Broch.

He decided to go out and warn the lad to sit down and behave himself, worried that the station would be getting an unfavourable mention in the traditional doom, death and disaster Monday-morning front page of *The Press and Journal*.

"Ye'll hae tae stan back fae the edge o the platform," he told the drunk. "There's a train comin shortly."

The drunk tried hard to focus on the railman and, swaying gently to left and right, slurred: "Ye're surely affa feart for yer trainie."

PASSENGERS ON the BA1301 Aberdeen–Heathrow flight one July morning in 2002 heard the following cabin announcement as their aircraft turned at the end of the runway, the noise of the engines began building and the plane began rolling towards take-off.

"There you go, ladies and gentlemen. As one bad egg said to the other bad egg: 'We're aff.'"

BACK TO 1984, now, and the height of the miners' strike. The Thatcher Government had authorised the use of every means possible to import foreign coal to maintain energy supplies, while Arthur Scargill and the National Union of Mineworkers were equally determined to prevent any such imports.

When word got round that a couple of boatloads of coal were arriving from Poland at Fraserburgh Harbour or one of the other wee harbours on the knuckle of Buchan, a busload of flying pickets was dispatched northwards by strike control.

According to John Henderson, of Bridge of Don, the Central Belt pickets got there just in time to see the dockworkers set about unloading the coal. The strikers were furious.

"You can't do that," they said. "That's black cargo."

"I wyte," said one dock worker, waving aside the protests, "I've nivver seen coal ony ither colour."

The Tales That Got Awa

Once again, here are the stories that arrived in the mail and which didn't have quite the same ring of truth as all the others. They were too good to waste, though. With the customary warning that you enter this section at your own risk, go ahead.

BACK TO the 1950s again, and the skating pond at Alford, where the locals used to hold ambitious skating contests while their curling counterparts had their bonspiels at the curling pond nearby.

At one such festival, a trio of judges was to be brought in from outside to lend a grander air to proceedings, but only the judge from Aberdeen and the judge from Elgin turned up, so Wullie, an unwitting local, was pressed into service as the third judge.

As Mina from Craigievar did her stuff on the rink, she stumbled once or twice. When the time came for the marks, the Aberdeen judge held up the boards showing 4 and 7. The Elgin judge held up 4 and 9. Wullie held up the maximum 6 and 0.

When the two expert judges queried his top marks, Wullie said: "I ken she hytered a puckle times, bit ye've tae myn it's affa skytie oot there."

A COUNTRY doctor was woken one night in the Fifties. At the other end of the phone was a panicky woman. "Oh, doctor, doctor," she cried. "Ye'll hae tae come. Ma man's deein!"

"Your husband's dying?" said the doctor. "What makes you think that?"

"It's affa skytie oot there."

"He's rollin aboot in the bed moanin and he's come oot in an affa sweat. I canna get ony sense oot o him ava."

The patient was a well-known drouth in the village, and the doctor was reluctant to climb out of a cosy bed for what he knew would be a waste of time, especially on a foul November night, so he calmed down the caller and said: "Have you got a barometer?"

"Aye, we hiv."

"Well, just you go and put the barometer on your husband's chest, watch the needle for a few hours to be sure he's all right, and come and see me in the morning." The woman promised she would do precisely that, and the doctor settled back to continue his sleep.

He was just drifting off half an hour later when the phone rang again. It was the same woman. "Oh, doctor, doctor. I can only thank ye."

"Thank me?" said the doctor. "Is your husband all right now?"

"Aye, yer barometer advice did the trick. I put it on his chest and the needle said Affa Dry, so I gied him a dram and noo he's sleepin like a bairn."

OUR POLICE contact, whose tip-offs appear in other chapters, also tried to persuade us that the Queen Street front desk in Aberdeen once took a call from an elderly Aberdonian man who wanted to report that his next-door garden was occupied by a shapely blonde in her early twenties who appeared to be sunbathing topless and wearing only a G-string.

"What do you expect us to do about that?" the desk sergeant said.

"I'm nae expectin ye tae dee onythin aboot it," the pensioner said. "I jist wintit tae tell somebody."

A HUNTLY man went to his doctor complaining of feeling sore all over. Every time he pressed his chest, it hurt. Every time he pressed his side, it hurt. Every time he pressed his neck, it hurt.

The doctor examined him and said: "You've broken your finger."

WE WERE both assured that at the height of the Tupperware craze in the North-east, one enterprising saleswoman promised that the next catalogue would contain Tupperware underwear. With her customers' curiosity piqued, she would add: "It disna dee muckle for yer shape, but it keeps fit ye've got fine and fresh."

THE LATE Sandy Benzie used to tell a story of a simple Deeside lad who attended the Aboyne Games every year because he liked the sideshows and amusements. On one such outing, he tried his hand at the shooting gallery and won himself a tortoise. Off he went to the beer tent to celebrate.

Emboldened by John Barleycorn, he returned to the shooting gallery an hour or two later and announced to the attendant: "See's anither go o yer sheetin, bit I'm nae sikkin nae mair o yer pies. The last een wis fine an sappy inside, bit it hid a maist damnable hard crust."

TO THE old Fine Fare supermarket at Bridge of Dee now, when Wullie and Erchie's trolleys collide. "Sorry aboot 'at," says Wullie. "I wisna lookin far I wis gaun. I've lost ma wife."

"That's a coincidence," says Erchie. "I've lost mine an aa and I'm getting a bittie desperate, for she gets terrible ratty if she thinks I'm nae keepin up wi her."

"Well," Wullie says, "maybe I've seen her. Fit dis she look like?"

"Well, she's 24, lang blonde hair, blue een, mini skirt, and leather beets up til her backside," says Erchie. "Fit dis yours look like?"

"Nivver mind," Wullie says. "We'll look for yours."

BACK IN the 1960s, an elderly Aberdeen couple were moved out of their tenement in George Street and rehoused in the new council tower-block flats at Cairncry.

One evening, the woman gave her man his tea then left the flat without saying where she was going.

She returned the following morning. Her man was speechless and she was near breathless herself.

"Thank God," she said. "That's my day for the stairs past."

THE STORY goes that when the Queen visited Aberdeen in 1964 as a signal to the world that the infamous typhoid epidemic was over and that the city was now perfectly safe, one of her stops included a visit to the Prosthetics Department at Aberdeen Royal Infirmary, where artificial limbs were being sculpted.

Her Majesty paused by one busy workman and inquired: "What exactly are you making here?"

He looked up. "Aboot 15 bob an oor."

YOU CAN send your complaints and groans to Ian Murray, of Macduff, who tried to tell us that he went into the Chinese supermarket in George Street, Aberdeen, and asked for canned pigeon.

"Sorry," said the assistant. "No can doo."

A KINTORE woman was lying on her deathbed. "Wullie," she said to her man, "I've ae last request. I ken ye've nivver likit ma sister, but jist for the look o the thing wid ye let her sit aside ye in the front car on the wye tae the ceemetry. Efter aa, she's ma only faimly."

"Weel," Wullie said, "Aaricht. Seein it's yer last request, I'll agree. Mind, it'll spile ma hale day."

THE name o Cocky Hunter, Aberdeen's legendary merchant, needs little introduction, but the story goes that perhaps some of his customers were not quite so aware of how good an eye Cocky had for a genuine antique.

A chap bowled up on a push-bike at the premises, wanting to see if Cocky was interested in what was supposedly a Van Gogh he had found in an outhouse.

Cocky called upstairs: "Wullie, foo mony Van Goghs hiv we got up there?"

"Five," came a voice.

"Twa poun for't." Cocky told the man, who accepted with very bad grace.

A few months later, the would-be art dealer turned up on his push-bike again, this time with a supposed Constable.

"Wullie," Cocky cried upstairs. "Foo mony Constables hiv we got up there?"

"Sivven," came the voice.

"Thirty bob," Cocky said. Again, the man grumbled, but took the cash.

A few months later, he turned up again with a small wooden sphere. "Fit's that?" Cocky inquired.

"It's a testicle aff the widden horse o Troy," the man said. "And afore ye speir at Wullie up there, I've got the ither een in ma pooch."

A NOTE from Inverurie told of a retired Garioch farmer who shuffled into the medical practice complaining that his love life was not what it had been. The doctor prescribed Viagra and asked the old boy to come back in two weeks.

A fortnight later, the consulting-room door opened and there stood the patient with a broad smile on his face and a spring in his step. He pirouetted in and sat down.

"Weel," said the doctor, "There's no need to ask how you're getting on. I can see for myself. It's written all over your face. Tell me, what does your wife think?"

"Couldna tell ye. Hinna been hame yet."

ALSO AT Inverurie was the man who offered a conversation lozenge to his mother, only for her to find that there was no writing on it.

When she brought this to his attention, he replied that he had scraped off the message deliberately as he wasn't speaking to her.

A SPINSTER went to her solicitor to make her will. She wanted half left to the Kirk and half to the man who could show her what she had been missing all these years.

"And who might the man be?" inquired the solicitor.

"I wis thinkin you," the spinster said.

"Mercy, but I'm a married man," the solicitor said. "And I've got family."

"Jist you awa hame and think aboot it. Discuss it wi yer wife."

Initially, his wife was having none of it, but she reasoned by morning that the money would come in handy, provided it was just the once and he was home by midnight.

Well, midnight came, then 1am, then 2am, 3am and 4am. By the time her man arrived home from his wee dalliance, she was furious.

"Now, now, Jean," he cautioned. "Haud yer tongue. The Kirk's nae gettin a penny."

THE TALE that came closest to appearing in a chapter of true stories was this one from Mintlaw, but ultimately we decided to play safe and place it here. The story goes that an elderly chap was making a call to the operator at the phone box in the middle of the town.

The operator said she wasn't able to help at that

moment, but if the caller was able to hang around in the box for a moment or two, she would do what she could to find him an answer and call him straight back.

As our caller hung up, another man appeared outside the box, clearly in a hurry. The original caller stepped outside and offered to let the other man use the phone if he was going to be quick. The second man accepted graciously and stepped inside the newly vacated phone box. Just as he was poised to make his call, however, the phone rang. Puzzled, he lifted the receiver.

"Hello," the operator said, "Are you the gentleman I was speaking to earlier?"

"Na," said the man. "I doot ye've got a wrang number."

"I don't think so," the operator said. "The call was definitely made from that number. Could the caller be standing outside, maybe?"

The man looked round and spied the first chap. "Hing on a mintie," said the man in the phone box. "I think I can maybe help ye. Wis he weerin broon sheen and a tweed jaicket?"

PERHAPS THE most implausible story that came our way was from Bill Robertson, of Newtonhill, who insisted a little too earnestly that it was true.

Shortly before he retired from what he described as "a humdrum career among lowlifes in the law", which we assume meant the people he apprehended rather than his colleagues in blue, Bill was hosting a charity trip to Edinburgh Zoo.

He spotted an elderly gentleman tossing £10 notes into the chimps' enclosure. When Bill asked what he thought he was doing, the man pointed at a nearby sign:

DO NOT FEED THESE ANIMALS BANANAS.
£10 FINE.

AND FINALLY, the joke that came at us from so many directions and from so many people that it deserves to have the honour of closing the book.

(Drum roll)

What do you call a Scotsman wearing Arab head-dress, a long white cloak and leading a camel across the Sahara?

Lawrence of Kemnay.

Where Credit's Due

ONCE AGAIN, we can take hardly any of the credit for the stories you have read in the book. Many have come from our daily activities in newspapers and on the radio, but just as many arrived by post from fowk across the North-east, throughout the rest of the country, aye, and a dozen or so from the far-flung corners of the globe, forbye.

To the best of our knowledge, they are true, apart from those we have flagged up clearly as wee works of fiction that were too good to throw away.

We thank everyone who took the time and trouble to write to us or who stopped us in the street, and especially the ones who said that they liked the first two books. We feel we can at least record these contributions, whether we had the space to use them or not.

If we have missed out anyone in the hurry to get the book ready, we're sorry.

Thanks to: Alison Harper, Esma Shepherd, Helen Hendry, Johnnie Duncan, T. Munro Forsyth, Douglas Schaske, Christine Birnie, Ethel Baird, Doug Hampton, Geordie Stott, the Reverend Jim Scott, Robert Adam, Jimmie Mitchell, Charles Barron, V.B. Taylor, R.P. Nicol, A.J. Harper, Mabel Mutch, James Morrison, Frances Patterson, Duncan Downie, Leslie and Hilda, Kenny Mackie, Donald Manson, Norman Harper Sen., Joan Christie, Ethel Simpson, Lindy Cheyne, Hamish Watt, Leslie Innes, Leslie Wheeler, Nan Sandison, Douglas Mutch, Lilianne Grant Rich,

Rena Gaiter, Gordon Milne, Graham Maclennan, Chrissabel Reid, John Stewart, Mary Riddoch, Bob Knowles, Andrew Foster, Bill Connon, Harry Walker, Norman Duncan, Sheila Knox, Isobel and Peter Slater, Douglas Merson, Norah Hardy, Violet Thomson, Yvonne Cormack, Jess Robertson, Donald McAllister, Jim Glennie, J.O. McHardy, Elizabeth Hendry, Bill Mowat, Elma Massie, Ian Dawson, Donnie McBeath, Ronnie Watson, Helen Mills, Bill Pirie, Frances Robb, Janice Cottier, Jim McColl, Mary Gerrie, Eric Wilson, Karen Buchan, Nanny and Hilda, Joe Watson, John Dear, George Durward, David Ross, Eileen Dunn, Sheila Innes, Billy Mathers, Dr Pat Macdonald, Jimmy Irvine, Bill Shand, Kathie Ross, the Reverend Gordon Smith, the Reverend Charles Birnie, Margaret Mathison, Sandy Matheson, Frances Jaffray, Sandy Watt, Lorna Alexander, Jimmy Murdoch, Allan Barnett, Ackie Manson and dozens of others who wrote and requested anonymity, as well as thousands who, over the years, have entertained us with their conversation.

Norman Harper and Robbie Shepherd
Aberdeen, 2004

BIRLINN LTD (incorporating John Donald and Polygon) is one of Scotlandís leading publishers with over four hundred titles in print. Should you wish to be put on our catalogue mailing list **contact**:

Catalogue Request
Birlinn Ltd
West Newington House
10 Newington Road
Edinburgh EH9 1QS
Scotland, UK

Tel: + 44 (0) 131 668 4371
Fax: + 44 (0) 131 668 4466
e-mail: info@birlinn.co.uk

Postage and packing is free within the UK. For overseas orders, postage and packing (airmail) will be charged at 30% of the total order value.

For more information, or to order online, visit or website at **www.birlinn.co.uk**

Birlinn